Shawn & Carla Anderson

Prescriptions for Troubled Hearts

Prescriptions FOR Troubled Hearts

Devotional Thoughts from the Psalms

by
Jim Mankin

GOSPEL ADVOCATE COMPANY
Nashville, Tennessee 37202

PRESCRIPTIONS FOR TROUBLED HEARTS

Printed in the United States of America

ISBN 0-89225-273-1

For
My Mother and Dad
who comforted me from many
a troubled heart.

Contents

Preface

We live in a world of intense uncertainty, fraught with many personal upheavals. It is always a "crisis situation" of some kind or other that moves us into active concern. The news rarely seems good any more, and the basic social structure of the family is crumbling. Yet in all of the maze of things, it is the individual that is in peril. It is to these hearts that are troubled that I choose to speak.

Even as I write these lines, one of my best friends lies in a hospital room the victim of an unsuspected malignancy. How swift a family's dream is shattered with this anxiety, and how quickly the person realizes anew that we live only one day at a time. No one can predict when such illness will strike, or some other heart-rending tragedy. Such days seem to almost never end, and the nights are longer and very lonely.

Most of us know the reality of troubled hearts, but where do we go for help? I have long believed that the ancient Psalms of David, and other writers, help to give us the prescriptions that we need. Over and over, I have read the Psalms, memorized some of them, turned to favorite ones for re-reading, and studied choice verses. I still marvel at the insights of these people who were so like us in today's busy and frustrated world.

So I began to develop these thoughts, collecting material and helps in an effort to give people the relief that they need. I have used them as the basis of many lessons and sermons, but I find that I turn to them more often in times of grave illnesses and to comfort those in sorrow. It is my hope that these will bring hope and spiritual health to your life also.

My appreciation is expressed to my wife, Deloris, and to my children for their patient care. I will be forever grateful to my secretary, Mrs. Shirley Ward, for not only her skill in typing the manuscript, but for her remarkable ability to be able to read my writing and most often anticipating my thoughts. A special word of gratitude goes to Lewis and Leota Maiden, English scholars and grammarians, who kindly read the manuscript and offered many valuable suggestions. Most of all, I am grateful to the Heavenly Father for his overshadowing providence throughout this project.

Jim Mankin
Madison Church of Christ
Madison, Tennessee

1. Blessed

"Blessed is the man . . . ."

PSALM 1:1

Many scholars say the book of Psalms is the most universally loved book in all the Bible. It has been a favorite for centuries, for the Jewish people used it as their song and prayer book. The early Christians also used it in worship, and many people have memorized their favorite Psalms. It was the third book printed in America.

The book of Psalms is unique, and this may explain the reason for its popularity. It is the only book that contains man's words addressed to God. We usually think of the Bible as being God's words to man. So, in this unusual book, we see glimpses into the inner religion of some of Israel's souls. Even though David wrote more of the Psalms than any other writer, others did write them also. The superscriptions have been added at the top of the Psalms to identify the author.

The first Psalm has been called "a threshold Psalm." It contains the theme of the entire book. Two ways are presented: the way of blessing and the way of cursing. It is for us to choose the way that we wish to go.

The Way of Blessing

It is significant that the Psalm opens with the word "blessed." Real happiness is always from God. Another translation says, "Oh, the happiness of the man!"

We remember that Jesus began his famous Sermon on the Mount with the Beatitudes. In eight instances of the qualities that his people were to possess, he began with the word "blessed." To be blessed is the idea and dream of this book. In a nutshell, the Psalms say there are only two ways—God's way or the way of nothing.

First, the portrait of the godly man is painted for us to see, and, hopefully, to emulate. He is pictured at the outset in a negative way. He does not *walk* in the counsel of the ungodly. This means he refuses to expose himself to the ideas and attitudes of men who have no place for God in their lives. The quality that we are seeking is godliness.

He does not *stand* in the way of sinners. He refuses to stop and associate himself with the rebellious offenders. To do so would mean a loss of the sensitivity to sin.

He does not *sit* in the seat of the scornful. The blessed man refuses to sit with those who sneer and scoff at the truth and sacred things. A scorner is nothing more than a cynic and a critic! He is to be avoided at all costs.

It is easy to notice in the Psalmist's description the progression of sin. First, is walking by sinners. Next, is standing with them. And finally, is sitting with them. This is the same thought that James gave us as Christians. He said that "each man is tempted, when he is drawn away by his own lust, and enticed. Then the lust, when it hath conceived, beareth sin: and the sin, when it is full-grown, bringeth forth death" (James 1:14-15). The thing that you need to ask yourself today is, "Where am I? Where is my child? Where is my mate? Am I going in the direction of embracing sin or am I steering away from it?" The old song is right:

Yield not to temptation,
For yielding is sin,
Each victory will help you,
Some other to win.

Then the blessed man is presented in a positive way. The Psalmist says that he delights in the law of the Lord. The truly happy person realizes that his source of strength is from God. He loves to read and meditate on the Bible. He fills his mind with the good thoughts that come from the scripture. It is so much easier when our lives are filled with beautiful things to remain pure and close to God, but the Psalmist also gives a vivid picture, in the words, "He shall be like a tree planted by the streams of water, that bringeth forth its fruit in its season." The suggestion here is of vitality, steadfastness, security, and fruitfulness. The truly happy person is like an evergreen. His leaf does not wither with the changing of seasons or climates of life. But whatever he does prospers and succeeds. God is behind him in seeing that he achieves an overall prosperity. Look at the beauty and the strength of the tree that grows by the river's bank, and you have a picture of what God thinks of the happy blessed man.

The Way of Cursing

The other side of the canvas reveals the wicked man. The Psalmist says emphatically, "The ungodly are not so." They refuse in their lives to let God live in them. They are guided by their own stubborn will. Instead of prospering, they are like the chaff that the wind blows away. Instead of being the good wheat that can be ground and used, they are just chaff. Their lives are meaningless, empty and vain. The trouble is that they have no foundation.

The final result is seen in the judgment. The wicked shall not stand in the judgment, for they will perish. How sad to come to the end of life with nothing to show for it. Jesus made the same point in the story of the two builders that closed his famous sermon. The wise man built on a rock, while the foolish man built his house on the sand. In the storms and pressures of life, the house built on the sand fell, while the house built on the rock stood. But the Lord added, concerning the house on the sand, "and great was the fall of it." A ruined life, ending tragically, brings great destruction to the person and heartache to all who have known him.

These six verses reveal to us two ways: Which way shall it be for you and me?

2. Consider

> "When I consider thy heavens . . . . what is man, that thou art mindful of him?"
>
> PSALM 8:3-4

The eighth Psalm has been called the "Psalm of the religious scientist." Another description of it is "a lyric echo of the first chapter of Genesis." If you are to understand and appreciate this Psalm, you must look carefully at four key words: name, consider, man, and dominion.

Name

"O Lord, Our Lord, how excellent is thy name in all the earth." The Psalm both opens and closes with this expression of praise. It is a truth that we all need to acknowledge in our lives—the greatness and majesty of God. Even God had it as one of his Ten Commandments, "Thou shalt not take the name of the Lord, thy God, in vain" (Exod. 20:7). God's name is set apart from all other names. It is to be revered and held in awe. Our Lord taught us to pray, "Our father, who art in Heaven, hallowed be thy name."

In the Old Testament, there are two basic roots of God's name that were very meaningful to the people. The first is the expression "El" or "Elohim." The meaning here is of power or the strong one. He is called EL Shaddai, meaning God Almighty, in Genesis 17:1. He is referred to as EL Roi, the God who sees, in Genesis 16:13, and for us he is still the Almighty, the one who sees and hears our needs.

The other expression is "Yahweh" or Jehovah. This is translated in the King James Version as "the Lord," but the Jews referred to it as THE NAME. For the Jewish people, it was such a sacred and holy name that they referred to him only as The One whose name cannot be pronounced. It was with this meaning that God told Moses his name was "I AM, THAT I AM" (Exod. 3:14). The meaning here is to be, for God is without creator, and he is beyond time. He has always existed and always will. Other uses of his name in this way are Jehovah-Jire, meaning "the Lord will provide," in Genesis 22:14; Jehovah-Nissi, meaning "Jehovah is my banner," in Exodus 17:15; and Jehovah-Shalom, meaning "Jehovah is peace," in Judges 6:24. In each case, we are still reminded of God's protection and care in our lives.

I like the story of the little boy who, in praying the model prayer, said, "Our Father who lives in New Haven, how do you know my name?" He was arriving close to the truth that God is interested in every person wherever he is, and does know our names.

Consider

Consider means to reflect upon, to think, to meditate. We sometimes sing, "Take time to be holy, speak oft with thy Lord." The Psalmist calls upon us here to consider God's works in nature. It is a night scene, one of stars and the moon. The earth is one planet out of nine revolving around the sun; yet the sun is one star in a galaxy called the Milky Way, which is 100,000 light years long. How long is a light year? The distance that light can travel in one year is 5,879-trillion miles. So the distance across the Milky Way is 587.9 quadrillion miles, and the Milky Way is only one of billions of galaxies. When we consider such awesome figures and expanse, we begin to wonder what is man that God is mindful of him.

David uses the poetic expression, "The work of thy fingers." David believed in the God of creation, but he also believed that we who live can worship and praise God because of his creation.

Man

With this view of the majesty of God, David then turned to the dignity of man. His question is, "What is man, that thou art mindful of him? And the Son of man, that thou hast visited him?" I believe that man was created in the very image of God. But more than this, I believe that God has made it possible for us to become his children through obedience to his son. God is interested in man infinitely more than he is in his creation, and even later the Psalmist declares that he does care for all of it.

I like the little children's song that expresses such a rich thought in this connection. Think on these words written by Johann Hay,

> Can you count the stars of evening,
> That are shining in the sky?
> Can you count the clouds that daily
> Over all the world go by?
> God, the Lord, who doth not slumber,
> Keepeth all the boundless number:
> But He careth more for thee,
> *But He careth more for thee.*

Man is crowned with glory and honor as a king. In fact, he is a little lower than the angels, or even as one translation puts it, a little lower than God himself. God is mindful of man and has given him an exalted place in the whole of the universe.

When we think of such love, we immediately think of the fact that God sent his only begotten son to the world to save us. It was because he thought our souls were worth saving.

Dominion

Man's dominion is over all of God's physical creation. All sheep, oxen, birds, and fish are under man's control. It is a God-given responsibility and covers many areas. The Psalmist believes that there is dignity to the work of man, that you and I are important, not only to God, but in the order and running of this physical universe. We have dominion over all the works of God's hand! We attain self-mastery by being mastered by God.

There is a marvelous footnote to this Psalm in the expression found in the eighth verse, "Whatsoever passeth through the paths of the sea." Many years ago, Matthew Fontaine Maury was sick at home, and he asked his son to read to him from the Bible. The son chose to read the eigth Psalm. When they got to this expression, Maury asked his son to read it again, which the son did. Then he said if the Bible says that there are paths in the sea, there must be paths in the sea, and I will find them. So it is, that this man is credited with being the founder of Oceanography and is now numbered in the Hall of Fame. He took the Bible at its word, and discovered what had been there all along. I often wonder how many other things are locked in this earth as secrets that man still can discover and know that he has the power to use them and harness them for good and for God's glory.

3. Model

"Jehovah, who shall sojourn in thy tabernacle? Who shall dwell in the holy hill?"

PSALM 15:1

I remember reading once about Phyllis McGinley, famous author and poet, who received a call one day from the White House with an invitation for dinner. She was ecstatic and thrilled, and eagerly accepted the invitation. But after she hung up the phone, she began to have second thoughts. The thoughts that kept running through her mind were, "What will I wear? What will I say to the President? Why did he invite me? Who else will be there?" With these kinds of thoughts, she nearly decided to write and decline the invitation, but finally she argued against that. For her it was a tremendous compliment to be invited to have dinner at the White House with the Chief Executive, and after the experience, she thoroughly enjoyed it.

As great as it would be to be invited to the White House, you and I are invited by God to ascend his holy hill and be in his presence. How do we prepare? What kind of person does he desire? In a sense, what must we wear to meet the Heavenly King?

People have answered this same question differently throughout the years. Some have thought that if one fasted, this would be pleasing to the Lord. Others have entered into the monastic life, removing themselves from society, living a life of meditation and prayer. One chief example of this was Simon, the Anchorite, who for 30 years lived on top of a flagpole. I suppose his motto was, "I shall not be moved." Others have said one must go through ritual and purification to meet God.

Yet the Psalmist makes a list of seven qualities that God requires, and they describe for us the model person. They are the kind of virtues that each of us can attain.

A General Description

The first quality is that God desires a person of integrity, one who loves righteousness (v. 2). This has to do with basic character, and God does look inside and read our hearts to see how we really are. This was the lesson that he taught the old prophet Samuel in the long ago when he was trying to anoint a king. Samuel was looking on the outward man, but God was looking on the inner heart. It was because of this that he chose David to be king after Saul.

During the Korean conflict, General William Dean was captured by the Communists. He was told that he could write a farewell letter to his family. General Dean was confident that after he wrote the letter, he would be shot. The letter contained only 8 or 9 lines, but to his only son, he wrote these words, "Tell Billy the word is *integrity*." When this man faced what he thought would be the end of his life, he did not have advice for Billy that the word was power, or money, or great influence. He said the word was integrity. He realized that it was a strength of character in the inner man that counted. I think for all of us the word is still integrity.

Second, God wants a man or woman who speaks the truth from deep down in his heart. It is still true that "as a man thinketh in his heart, so is he." When good and truth are part of our thinking process, this will be what we will speak.

Closely related to this is the third quality, which is for a person to be engaged in works of righteousness. The model person strives to be blameless before God. This means that everyday we have to live the life of goodness. Our daily life is marked by a certain walk or certain words, and certain works. This is to have sincerity without spot or wrinkle.

Specific Requirements

It is at this point, that the Psalmist makes specific recommendations. These are found in verses 3-5. All of these qualities are still attainable. The fourth he mentions is that the model person must refuse to let his tongue get out of control. A tongue out of control can injure an innocent bystander. God rebukes the slanderer, the talebearer, the defamer, and the gossiper. People can be sewer pipes to carry ugly and unfounded reports. It is still important to keep our tongue in control.

The fifth quality is that we must refrain from those who are evil. The model person does not do evil to a friend, nor does he take up reproach against a neighbor. In this same vein, we all despise a reprobate. We do not want to be around someone who can contaminate our lives. "Evil companionships corrupt good morals" (1 Cor. 15:33). On the other side, the model person honors those who honor the Lord.

Sixth, the model person keeps his word, no matter what the cost. At first reading, we may think that the Psalmist either wrote the wrong words, or there has been a misprint in our Bible. The passage says that the model person "sweareth to his own hurt, and changeth not" (v. 4c). This goes back to the old idea that used to be prevalent in our country, that a man's word was his bond. The classic Bible example of speaking and making a vow and not changing it is Jephthah, the Old Testament judge. He made a vow to God that he would offer the first thing that came out to greet him if God let him be victorious in the battle. Little did he realize that it would be his own daughter who would come out after that victory. Another example is of Daniel, who continued to pray to God three times every day, inspite of the king's decree that no one must ask of any power except the king only, for a period of days. We admire the courage and the faith of Daniel.

Seventh, the model person refuses to enrich himself at the expense of his neighbor. The question of usury or interest must be seen in the light of the 20-50 percent interest rate that was charged in that day. It was an unfair advantage especially against the poor. It is just not right to take advantage of other people when we try to loan money. A bribe is always wrong in that it perverts justice. How careful we have to be even with our material possessions and how we use them. They must be used for good and for righteousness.

The Psalmist says, "He that doeth these things shall never be moved." This is the reward that all of us can have. God is inviting you to dwell with him forever. These seven qualities give you the way that you can be the model person and live with him. Are you that person?

4. Nature

"The heavens declare the glory of God; and the firmament showeth his handiwork."

PSALM 19:1.

C. S. Lewis, the great English classicist, said of the 19th Psalm, "I take this to be the greatest poem in the Psalter and one of the greatest lyrics in the world."

The beauty of this Psalm is that it exalts God in nature, and God in his revelation. This is the book of nature and the book of revealed truth. In the former we see God's power, and in the latter his love. How majestically David begins this Psalm. The heavens declare the glory of God. It is as if the heavens are speaking and telling of God's glory to the whole human race.

In one of the hymns that we sing, there is the line, that says, "Beyond the sacred page I seek thee, Lord." This suggests that there is a way that we can know something of God through his creation. Even though he has revealed much to us in this Bible, we can see his power and greatness and genius in the created world. Truly the heavens declare! The firmament showeth!

As we read these opening lines of the 19th Psalm our minds are called back to the beginning of the Bible, with the impressive words, "In the beginning God created the heavens and the earth. . . . and God said, let there be light: and there was light" (Gen. 1:1,3).

In his book, *Psalms of David,* David Redding has written, "Creation is God's first sermon to us. It is the very first word he ever spoke, and he is not through pronouncing it. God's verbs in this universal language are planets, His nouns are suns, His dictionary is the milky way."

The Sun Is the Star

The greatest member of the heavenly choir is the sun, and is described by David as an athlete. In this day in which jogging is so prominent, we can imagine a person running for four or five miles, and seeing him exhibit strength and endurance. But as David views the sun, he sees the strong man running his course, from one end of the earth to the other. David uses the same language that we use; he saw the sun rise and set.

He also compared the sun to a bridegroom, one dressed up for a special occasion, shining in all of his brilliance. For most young men the wedding day is special, and perhaps never again looks and dresses as he does on that occasion. So the parallel is there, with the exception that the sun dresses daily for this pilgrimage across the sky. In brightness and in glory the sun comes up each day. The rays of the sun are so powerful that nothing is hid from its heat. And even now in the 1980's we are just beginning to tap the power of solar energy.

The Beauty of Morning

Really, I am a morning person. I love to get up early and go out and sit on the patio and look at the trees, and hear the birds sing and smell the flowers. And when it is not the season of the year that you can smell the flowers, there is still something awesome about the colors of the leaves in fall, and the silence of the snow in the winter. Perhaps, the Psalmist was expressing my feeling too when he wrote, "Oh Jehovah, in the morning shalt thou hear my voice; in the morning will I order my prayer unto thee, and will keep watch" (Ps. 5:3).

Maybe you too have had the feeling of wanting to go out and commune with nature early in the morning.

For me it just starts out the day to know that I have been protected through the night, have arisen to a new day with its opportunities before me, and have those few moments of silence and meditation before I begin in the hurry scurry of life. I suggest to you that you use for your motto each new day these words: "This is the day which the Lord has made; we will rejoice and be glad in it" (Psalm 118:24). It is marvelous to know that we have this day that we can use for God's glory.

The Night Also Speaks

Even though there is something wonderful about the beginning of the day and the power of the sun, when the sun has done its work, the night takes up the message. There are the moon and the stars that shine and twinkle. The marvelous thing is that God is letting us know in every way that he is with us and protecting us. I am intrigued when I learn that "He counteth the number of the stars; He calleth them all by their names" (Psalm 147:4).

Yet the speech of the sun, the moon and stars is enrapped in silence. Though they declare a message that is powerful, they have no human voice. And yet, their voice has gone throughout the whole world. In the silence that they proclaim there is a message that we can truly hear.

Perhaps Joseph Addison's hymn, "The Spacious Firmament on High," best expresses this beauty of God's work in nature.

> The spacious firmament on high,
> With all the blue, ethreal sky,
> And spangled heav'ns, a shining frame,
> Their great Original proclaim:

The unwearied sun from day to day
Does his Creator's power display,
And publishes to every land
The work of an almighty hand.

Soon as the evening shades prevail,
The moon takes up the wondrous tale,
And nightly to the listening earth
Repeats the story of her birth;
While all the stars that round her burn,
And all the planets in their turn,
Confirm the tidings as they roll,
And spread the truth from pole to pole.

What tho' in solemn silence all
Move round this dark terrestrial ball?
What tho' no real voice nor sound
Amid their radiant orbs be found?
In reason's ear they all rejoice,
And utter forth a glorious voice,
For ever singing as they shine,
"The hand that made us is divine."

5. Bible

"Oh how love I thou law! It is my meditation all the day."

PSALM 119:97.

I love the Bible. From my earliest childhood the Bible has been a special book in my life. Even before I could read it myself, it occupied a treasured place in our home, and my mother read to me the stories from it. As I grew older I learned to respect it, memorize the books of it, and sing about it. It means more to me now than it has ever meant.

It is evident when you read the book of Psalms that the Psalmist also thought of the Bible as a special book. To him it was God's word. As God's word it was to be desired more than gold, and it is sweeter than honey.

The 19th Psalm really has two parts, the first part exalts God's work in nature, while the latter half exalts the word of God. In many ways the 19th and the 119th Psalm (the longest Psalm which exalts the word) are explanations of the truth found in the first Psalm, that the man of God delights in the law of the Lord.

The Many Sided Revelation

These words that describe the Bible are interesting to note in the direction in which they go, based on Psalm 19:7-14.

1. The Law.

"The law of Jehovah is perfect, restoring the soul."

This is the chief term of all and is heard and used most

often. It comes from a word that means to teach or to direct. It reminds that revelation is not simply for our own interests or enjoyment, but for our obedience. When we look in the perfect law of liberty, we have to remember that we have to be doers of the word. Compare James 1:25.

2. Testimonies.

"The testimony of Jehovah is sure, making wise the simple."

The people of God were told in the long ago to place the book of the law beside the ark of the covenent "that it may be there for a witness against you" (Deut. 31:26). The scripture warns, and sets a high standard for our living, and is often outspoken, but it remains the true and faithful witness. We can be sure that God's testimonies are right.

3. Precepts.

"The precepts of Jehovah are right, rejoicing the heart."

This word is drawn from the idea of an overseer, a man who is responsible to look into the situation and take action. This word points to the particular instructions of the Lord, and shows the detail with which God is concerned.

4. Statutes.

"The statutes of the Lord are right, rejoicing the heart."

This speaks of the binding force and permanence of the scripture. It has been engraven for all time. God's statutes stand.

5. Commandments.

"The commandment of Jehovah is pure, enlightening the eyes."

This emphasizes the authority of what God has said. he not only has the right to try to persuade us, he has the authority to give the orders. We are always so much better off when we learn to obey his will. John, the apostle of love, reminded all of us that God's commandments are not grievous, in the sense of a burden that's too heavy, but rather if we love him, we will obey him. Compare 1 John 5:4.

6. Ordinances.

"The ordinances of Jehovah are true and righteous altogether."

God's way is right. We can rely upon his judgments and know that he is dealing fairly with us. Aren't we glad that he is the judge and not us, because we would make mistakes, and with him there are none.

7. Word.

"Thy word have I laid up in my heart, that I might not sin against thee" (Ps. 119:11.)

This is the most generally used term of all, and is one that we still employ today. God's word, the living, breathing word of God, teaches us the way of life. Oh, how we ought to love his word and realize that it is the book by which we will be judged. God's word is sweeter than honey, and to be desired more than gold. No wonder the Psalmist could exclaim, "Thy word is a lamp unto my feet, and light unto my path" (Ps. 119:105).

We can rely upon the promise of God in his word, and it will not be changed. God's word warns us of sins and problems. Yet, at the same time it tells us of the great hope of heaven and the reward for the righteous. But the promises truly come from his word.

Thomas Carlyle once wrote, "There is nothing solid to rest on but the faith which I learned in my old home, and from my mother's lips." Psalm 119:9 states the same truth, "Wherewith shall a young man cleanse his ways? By taking heed thereunto according to thy word."

On the wall of the old Park Street Church in Boston, A. Z. Conrad's tribute to the indestructibility of the Bible is engraved in bronze. The words are worth repeating:

Century follow century—There it stands.
Empires rise and fall and are forgotten—There it stands.
Dynasty succeeds dynasty—There it stands.
Kings are crowned and uncrowned—There it stands.

Emperors decree its extermination—There it stands.
Atheists rail against it—There it stands.
Agnostics smile cynically—There it stands.
Profane prayerless punsters caricature it—There it stands.
Unbelief abandons it—There it stands.
Higher critics deny its claim to inspiration—There it stands.
The flames are kindled against it—There it stands.
The tooth of time gnaws but makes no dent in it—There it stands.
Infidels predict its abandonment—There it stands.
Modernism tries to explain it away—There it stands.

6. Forsaken

"My God, my God, why hast thou forsaken me?"

PSALM 22:1

It would seem that the Psalmist was sitting at the very foot of the cross when he wrote the words of the 22nd division of the book. Imagine in your own mind all the events surrounding the crucifixion, and then try to comprehend the agony and suffering of our Lord. Not only is Jesus dying for the sins of the world; he is dying to save you and me. If for no other reason than the theme of the cross, we would love this particular Psalm.

The Cry

Jesus on the cross felt the loneliness of death. He felt the abandonment of God. Thus, he raised the cry of *"Why?"*

Why is a word of mystery. The people in the days of Haggai, the prophet, wondered *why* they did not have sufficient crops. The reason was that God was displeased with their lack of commitment to his cause (Hag. 1:9). In the ministry of Jesus, the disciples were asked by a concerned father to cast out the demons in his son. Yet they could not do it. They asked the question of the Lord, *"Why* could we not cast it out?" (Matt. 17:19). Jesus asked the Jews of his day, "If I say truth, *why* do you not believe me?" (John 8:46). Still the Lord speaks and says, "And *why* call ye me, Lord, Lord, and do not the things which I say?" (Luke 6:46).

In the case of Jesus on the cross, his "why hast thou

forsaken me" rises from a troubled heart and from honest doubt. He doesn't understand. He feels completely forsaken, but he still says, "*My God,* why hast thou forsaken me?" We feel that we are taken into the very mind and body of the sufferer, and we can feel what Jesus felt.

His pathetic cry on the cross reminds us again of the humanness of the Lord. One of his other expressions was, "I thirst." We understand that physically he thirsted and just wanted a cool drink of water. But the cry from the cross about being forsaken is a deep longing of the soul!

At the actual moment of death, God had turned his back on Jesus. After all, Jesus was the symbol of sin. He was taking our place. The Bible declares, "While we were yet sinners, Christ died for the ungodly" (Rom. 5:8). Thus, God turned from him because he represented all that was sin.

Yet, Jesus becoming the sin offering shows his complete obedience to the will of God. He made the supreme sacrifice in order that he could save us. It was really God's will, for it was in his eternal plans to have his son slain for the sins of the world.

Once a lady came to J. W. McGarvey, the noted Bible scholar. She asked this probing question, "Where was God when my son died?" Brother McGarvey thought for awhile and gave her this answer, "I suppose he was in the same place when your son died as he was when his own son died."

To feel forsaken by God was to know the agony of hell itself. When you feel that you have been forsaken by friends and family, you also know the bitter experience of defeat and discouragement. Yet, we too can cry out to God and know that he listens and hears. This is made available because of the atonement of his son in our behalf. To reject his love, means that you must face the darkness of the night that the Lord went through.

The Mockings

Our Lord was scorned by men and despised by the people. It is in this sense that he felt his humility and holiness, so that he could express in the words of the Psalmist, "But I am a worm, and no man; a reproach of men, and despised of the people" (v. 6). He was an object of derision. How would we like it if someone looked at us, wagging his head in disbelief of our innocence, if others would even spit in our face, and still others would slap us with the palm of their hand? Yet, this is what the Lord went through on our behalf.

"All they that see me laugh me to scorn: they shoot out the lip, they shake the head, saying, He trusted on the Lord that he would deliver him: let him deliver him, seeing he delighted in him" (vv. 7, 8).

This basically is what the people said to Jesus while he was hanging on the cross, suffering and dying. Even the chief priest entered the fracas and said *if* he were the son of God, God would give him the power to come down from the cross. Is it any wonder that even the robbers who were hung on the cross began to rebuke him also?

The enemies of the Lord are described by the Psalmist as bulls, lions, dogs, a company of evildoers. What kind of effect does this harassment have on the Lord?

This caused the Lord's physical condition to be miserable. To use again the words of the Psalmist, he was "poured out like water," his "bones are out of joint," his "heart is like wax," his "strength is dried up like potsherd," and his "tongue cleaves to his jaws."

Even while on the cross, the soldiers cast lots for the garments of Jesus, which was prophesied in verse 18. Nothing was sacred—not even his seamless robe!

Men are still using the same tactics on us that they used on our Lord and Master. It may well be that we have to suffer in some degree as he did. But it's still hard to take when people speak unfairly about us. It's still difficult to hold back tears when they scorn with derision. But these mockings, if they are for righteousness sake, will earn us a reward.

The Triumph

The Psalmist declares that when he cried to God, he was heard (v. 24). Through the agony of the cross, Jesus suffered in order to reach the goal—to purchase the church with his own blood. Because of his goal, which involved the salvation of each person who would submit to his will, it was with a certain sense of joy in what he was doing that he endured. Perhaps the Psalmist expressed it best in the words, "For the kingdom is Jehovah's" (v. 28).

When we know that all things are in the Lord's hand, and that good and righteousness will triumph, we can endure, too. God is not deaf. He does hear our cries. He knows when we are suffering the mockery of friends or enemies.

It is because of the ultimate glory, that Jesus was able to die with a shout of his lips, "It is finished!" All four writers record that he cried with a loud voice, but it is only John who actually tells us what he said (John 19:30). When he said this, he was ready for God to receive his spirit. He died a victor! He passed through the valley of the shadow of death, but then he saw light. When he arose three days later from the dead, he brought salvation to us, as well as life eternal.

We may be forsaken for a time, but in Christ we will win.

7. Shepherd

"The Lord is my shepherd; I shall not want."

PSALM 23:1

Of all the Psalms in the Psalter, none is more beloved than the 23rd. It has been read, studied, memorized, and loved by countless millions of people. The simple majesty of its words thrill and inspire in a way that few words in all of literature have. Let us look at each phrase together again that we may enjoy its marvelous incite into living.

"The Lord is My Shepherd"

David, the author of this poem, was himself a shepherd. He begins with faith. Jehovah, the Lord God of Israel, is his shepherd. For the Christian, we can say that our shepherd is God's Son, Jesus. He told us that he was the good shepherd (John 10:11).

This simple profound statement implies a working relationship between a human being and his maker. The greater, the wider, the more majestic concept I have of Christ, the more vital my relationship with him will be.

I am the sheep; the Lord is the shepherd. Look at who is my owner, my manager. The difference is in the way that he manages me. I'm not just a part of a mob, with my own fears and stupidity to haunt me, but I am led by one who knows the way. I belong to him simply because he deliberately chose to create me as an object of his affection. Then at Calvary, he demonstrated the deeper desire to have me come unto his benevolent care. Isaiah wrote, "All we like sheep have gone astray; we've turned everyone to his own way; Jehovah has laid on him the iniquity of us all" (Isa. 53:6). Sheep cost money, and Jesus paid the price for me.

Because he owns me, he has put his mark on me. A shepherd normally marks his sheep in the ear, so that other shepherds would know that this one belongs to a certain flock. In a similar way Christ has marked me for his service. I cannot belong to another fold since I belong to him. Paul wrote, "Henceforth let no man trouble me; for I bear branded on my body the marks of Jesus" (Gal. 6:17).

"I Shall Not Want"

In the care of my shepherd, I shall not have a want since nothing is lacking. This is true because I am contented in my shepherd's care. David knew and had experienced this care, such as in the times that he had fled from Saul, and later when he had to flee from his own rebellious son, Absalom.

The management of the flock is wholly responsible for the welfare of the flock. This includes water, food, care, and protection. Uncared for, a sheep would likely escape. But because of the nature of a sheep, he would probably lose his way or be devoured by a wild animal. How dependent we are on our shepherd.

The shepherd is diligent. He has to be on the lookout for any trouble, constantly watching over the flock. "He will not suffer thy foot to be moved; he that keepeth thee will not slumber" (Ps. 121:3).

"He Maketh Me to Lie Down in Green Pastures"

Owing to their timidity, sheep refuse to lie down unless they are free of all fear. Even a rabbit jumping in front of one sheep can cause a stampede of the whole flock. The presence of the shepherd helps to overcome this fear. They will not lie down unless free from tension and rivalry among the flock. A peculiar thing about sheep is that they have a "butting order." An old ram might decide to move a younger lamb from a choice spot but when he sees the shepherd, he is content to go back to where he was. The more we know about sheep, the more they sound like people, and we can then see why the parallel is used in both covenants of scripture.

Sheep also must be free from the torment of parasites and insects. A shepherd uses chemicals to avoid this trouble and problem. Before they can lie down and rest in peace, they must have freedom from hunger. Green pastures were produced only from hard toil. Yet, if care is taken for the sheep's welfare, he can add as much as 100 pounds in 100 days from birth. On the other hand, if a sheep is ill-fed, it will continually wander in search of food.

Our shepherd is the kind that helps us to lie down in peace, in pastures that are green and full. We can only say with Paul, "For I have learned, in whatsoever state I am, therein to be content" (Phil. 4:11).

"He Leadeth Me Beside Still Waters"

Water is very important to sheep, since their bodies contain 70 percent water. If they do not find clean water, they will drink polluted water. This can create some tremendous problems, and the sheep often die.

Sheep can get water from the dew on the grass, early in the morning. They can also be led to wells of deep water for the shepherd to draw out the supply. Or they can be taken to clean springs and streams.

The problem with the sheep is that he has a nervous stomach and cannot drink from a bubbling brook. This is why the Psalmist emphasizes the still waters. We are reminded again of our own condition, that we often are nervous and in a state of confusion. But when we are led by God, he takes care of our needs in just the way that we can do best. He gives us living water.

"He Restoreth My Soul"

An old term for a sheep that is turned over on its back is a "cast sheep." The sheep is helpless in this condition. If the owner does not arrive on the scene in a short time, it will die. Not only does the shepherd keep a sharp eye on his sheep, but so do dogs, coyotes, and buzzards. The "cast sheep" is helpless, and often the one that falls and is turned over is the fattest sheep and thus the most valuable.

The circulation of the sheep does not work properly when he is in such a pathetic position, and the only thing the sheep knows to do is to kick his feet and bleat. This just makes his condition worse. The shepherd looks until he finds the sheep, rubs its legs, holds it close to his bosom, while gently talking to it all the while. He truly restores the sheep back to his life. In light of this, we can understand better Jesus' parable of the lost sheep. The shepherd was concerned about the one that was outside the fold, even though he had the 99 who were safe. Danger threatened the one that was away. One soul, like the one sheep, is valuable in the sight of our Lord.

"He Leadeth Me in the Paths of Righteousness for His Name's Sake"

Sheep are notorious creatures of habit, feeding in the same place over and over. They can even ruin a piece of ground simply by refusing to move. So the shepherd has to have a plan to work them to new areas and to continually rotate their feeding place.

We, too, need this advice of following our leader. He knows how to lead us in paths of righteousness. Instead of choosing our own way, we have to be willing to take the way of Christ. Will you be his sheep?

8. Surely

"Surely, goodness and mercy shall follow me all the days of my life."
PSALM 23:6

"*Yea, though I walk through the valley of the shadow of death, I will fear no evil, for thou art with me.*" The Psalmist has been talking of the shepherd's care, even boasting to his unfortunate neighbor, but now he turns to address the shepherd directly. The long trek into the high country has begun with the summertime. The sheep go on long drives, but they move slowly, eating gradually as they work their way up to the mountain. Then as the season changes into autumn, they begin to come back down so that they can be at the home ranch when the snow comes. Along the way are some valleys, some deep ravines that are scarred.

The Psalmist says the shepherd leads them *through* the valley. They do not have to stay *in* the valley. The same is true of our shepherd. We do not have to stay in the valley of the shadow of death. Our savior knows when we pass through these times, but he says to each of us, "And, lo, I am with you always, even to the end of the world" (Matt. 28:20).

Disappointment, tragedy, sickness, and death are all dark valley experiences. But we know that we must pass through these in order to reach safety at home. What comfort and reassurance to know that our shepherd knows the way we travel.

"Thy Rod and Thy Staff, They Comfort Me"

The shepherd's rod was a stick, carved to fit his hand with a bigger head on it. He practiced with it for hours, aiming at an object and throwing it there. The rod was a weapon of defense. Perhaps, no one has ever used his shepherd's rod in the ways that Moses did. God asked him, "What is in thy hand?" This simple object was then turned into a serpent. Later Moses stretched out his rod, the Red Sea parted, and the children of Israel crossed over safely.

But the shepherd's rod was also used for discipline, to correct some sheep, or one that was going to a poisonous weed. It could be used in the sense of setting a sheep back on the right path, even as a parent uses discipline for a child.

Shepherds also used their rods to examine and count their sheep. To come unto the shepherd's rod was to be carefully examined to determine the skin and the cleanness of the fleece. One does not pull the wool over the shepherd's eye. He sees and knows each sheep.

The staff was primarily the symbol of concern and compassion. It was a long slender stick with a crook at the end. The shepherd used his staff to lift a newborn lamb and then to bring it to his mother if they got separated. It was also used to reach out and catch individual sheep and draw them to him. It was further used for guiding the sheep by applying pressure to its side.

"Thou Preparest a Table Before Me in the Presence of Mine Enemies"

The high mountain ranges were referred to as "mesas," the Spanish word for table. This is what David refers to as the high plateaus. The shepherd, when he got the sheep to one of these tables, checked first for poisonous weeds and then took drastic steps to eradicate them. All of them had to be pulled up before it was safe for the sheep to have a meal.

Second, the shepherd had to keep his eyes open for predators. Wolves, coyotes, cougars and bears could be around. For the Christian, we realize that the devil is described as "a roaring lion, seeking whom he may devour" (1 Peter 5:8).

Our good shepherd has gone to great expense and trouble to prepare for us because he understands us, and he totally identifies with us. When we come to the Lord's table, what do we think about? We may be surrounded by every kind of enemy, but under the Lord's protection and watchful eye, we are safe.

"Thou Anointest My Head With Oil, My Cup Runneth Over"

Summertime is the time for flies. Sheep are especially bothered by the nose fly. They buzz about the head, attempting to deposit their eggs on the damp membranes of the sheep's nose. If successful, they form a wormlike larva and go inside the nasal passages and set up irritations. It's an agonizing time for the sheep. They have been known to beat their heads against trees and rocks and post. When the shepherd sees this display of pain, he immediately starts to do something to help.

The shepherd mixes up a solution—linseed oil, sulphur, tar—and applies this to the sheep's nose and head. When this is applied, the aggravation leaves. Summertime also brings scabs, a highly contagious disease when the sheep rub noses. It can go through a whole flock quickly. So, again the shepherd anoints the sheep with oil.

As children of God, we have the anointing of the Holy Spirit. We can feel God's goodness and can know of his love. Therefore, we exclaim, "My cup runneth over."

"Surely, Goodness and Mercy Will Follow Me All the Days of My Life."

The sheep have such a shepherd that they know that goodness and mercy will follow them wherever they go. It is almost as if David gets to the end of the Psalm and thinks of life with all of its cares and problems. He pauses, and then says, "surely." Surely, God will be good to us. Surely, his blessings will continue to flow. Surely, he will take care of us and give us everything we need. This is the kind of shepherd we have.

Yet, though his blessings flow to me, I too should have goodness and mercy following me as a blessing to others. Did you know that the sheep leaves behind a rich manure that benefits the soil? It can change a depressed land into one that is rich and green and fertile. What am I leaving behind me? Do I leave behind peace or turmoil? Forgiveness or bitterness? Contentment or conflict? Love or rancor?

"I Will Dwell in the House of the Lord Forever"

The whole Psalm closes with a positive statement. Fall has come and the shepherd starts his way home. The ultimate object is to get back home. If perchance winter comes quickly, the shepherd even uses wine to revive the sheep so that he can bring them the last mile home. For the child of God, our goal is to dwell in the house of the Lord forever. Our shepherd and owner cares about us, while Satan doesn't. You and I will be in the presence of the Saviour forever. When we understand this, we will bless his name. It is a certainty. Surely, goodness and mercy shall follow me all the days of my life, and *I will dwell in the house of the Lord forever*. Amen.

9. Fearless

"Jehovah is my light and my salvation;
whom shall I fear?
Jehovah is the strength of my life; of
whom shall I be afraid?"

PSALM 27:1

Once William Cowper was at a low point in his life. He boarded a cab in London and asked the cabbie to drive him to the river. His intention was to jump in. Life seemed meaningless, and he could not take any more of it.

However, the driver seemed to have lost his way with the fog of London, and he continued to drive aimlessly about for a long time. Finally, the cab stopped, and Cowper looked out to see that they were back at his own doorstep. He felt that this was providential, and so he went inside and wrote these moving words:

God moves in a mysterious way
His wonders to perform;
He plants His footsteps in the sea,
And rides upon the storm.

Judge not the Lord by feeble sense,
But trust Him for His grace;
Behind a frowning providence
He hides a smiling face.

All of us at times face disappointment, despair, and failure. We know that life is not always bright. But in such times, do we have a helper? When death is near, is there hope? The 27th Psalm that David wrote breathes with confidence.

The Sure Defense

David's confidence is in the Lord; therefore why should he fear? He believes that God is his light and salvation. Light is used here in the sense of the right path that God shows. God also is a refuge in time of danger.

We think of the time when David was fleeing for his life, when he was pursued by King Saul. He especially felt God's leadership and guidance. All of us need to know that we have such a refuge in time of danger. We still sing the words of Augustus Toplady's song,

> Rock of Ages, cleft for me,
> Let me hide myself in thee.

David experienced evil men, and so will we. These people who work evil are still in the world and are very active. But if we have trust in God, our fear will be removed. David said, "Though a host shall encamp against me, my heart shall not fear." As a young man, he had no fear when he faced Goliath, and now that he was older he still had nothing to fear. How wonderful it would be if everyone could understand that we can have this kind of confidence if we place our lives in the hand of God.

The Heart's Desire

In verse 4, David tells us the one desire that he has. This is the thing that he wants more than anything else from the Lord. He writes, "One thing have I asked of Jehovah, that will I seek after: that I may dwell in the house of Jehovah all the days of my life, to behold the beauty of Jehovah, and to inquire in his temple."

One of the reasons for David's confidence was that he not only had God as his helper, but he had the place to worship. You can have the same kind of confidence when you seek above everything else to do God's will. This was what Jesus meant when he said, "Seek ye first the kingdom of God and his righteousness, and all these things will be added unto you." This gives purpose and meaning to life.

All of us should have the desire to behold the beauty of the Lord, in the sense of being in his presence. Oliver Wendell Holmes once said, "There is a little plant within my heart called reverence. It must be watered at least once a week." What he was saying was that each of us needs to take time to worship God in an assembly at least once a week. For the true Christian it will be easy to find times to worship the Lord. Not only does it bring us in contact with the Lord and spiritual power, but worship puts us in association with the very best of people.

When we have the joy and privilege of worship, it keeps us constantly protected by the power of the Almighty. He has promised to hide us as a child would flee to his mother and go into the folds of her skirt.

The Cry of the Soul in Trouble

The mood of the Psalm changes and David cries out for help. He says, "Hear, O Jehovah, when I cry with my voice: have mercy also upon me and answer me." We all face temptations, and we must rely on God to help us.

The first lesson to be learned when we are in trouble is to seek the face of God. David understood this principle. He explained it thus, "Seek ye my face; my heart said unto thee, 'Thy face, Jehovah, will I seek' " (v. 8).

God desires our seeking. In fact, he has promised if we seek for his blessing, he will give it.

David felt so lonely and forsaken that he pleaded for God never to forsake him and turn from him. At this particular point in his life, he even felt that his parents had left him alone. Some of us have come to such times in our life when we felt that we were completely alone in the world, that no one cared. The easiest thing for us would be to resign from the human race. If there were only some way that we could silently slip away from the scene of life, for no one seems to care. But it's in times like these that we do have a helper. The almighty God who made us knows and will understand the way in which we go. David believed that "then Jehovah will take me up."

True, David was ready to faint. He was at the end of his rope. He would have given up, unless he had believed. His words here were most perceptive: "I had fainted, unless I had believed to see the goodness of Jehovah in the land of the living" (v. 13). He was almost down, and he had almost quit, but not quite. Fainting can be a common problem for all of us, yet if we hold on to our faith in the goodness of God, there is hope.

As Paul, the great apostle, wrote many years later to the Philippians (Phil. 4:19), "My God shall supply all of my (your) needs through Christ Jesus." So we have this confidence and this hope. We never have to fear when we place our trust in him. We can be fearless.

10. Forever

"Jehovah knoweth the days of the perfect; and their inheritance shall be forever."

PSALM 37:18

Everyone desires to live forever. We remember reading in history of the man Ponce de Leon and his search for the Fountain of Youth. He went many places; he followed every lead; he spent a lifetime and a fortune on this elusive goal of finding a famous fountain of water that would make him perpetually young.

In another age, a man named Graham made bread. He became so enamored with his bread, and the fact that it contained the best of ingredients, that he even advertised that if any person would eat Graham's Bread, he would live forever.

To live forever in this world would not be best, because there are so many problems. Yet, the desire to live is always present. Perhaps the real secret of living forever is to know how to live here so that we could enjoy an eternity forever. Some of the best advice in the scripture is found in the 37th Psalm. It is practical and down-to-earth about how to live, with the emphasis on *real living*. Yet the key to understanding this Psalm is verse 18, where David says, "The Lord knoweth the way of the perfect, and their inheritance shall be forever."

David is now old, and he is giving us the wisdom of his years. His rules for living are always simple, and therefore they have been bypassed by many. But if you would know the secret of living forever, stick with this Psalm and its advice.

Fret Not Because of Evildoers

The people who desire to live with God must learn this secret: do not be vexed or overheated about the wicked. David puts it so simply, "Fret not thyself because of evildoers, neither be thou enviest against them that work unrighteousness. For they shall soon be cut down like the grass, and wither as the green herb."

There is a tendency for all of us to worry about wicked people, and their prospering. We can't understand why they seem to be doing so well in comparison with the righteous. But what we fail to see is that there is a final day of reckoning coming.

An old story relates how two farmers with their property joining, approached life so differently. One man was a dedicated Christian and was rearing his family to honor God and the Bible. For him, the church and worship were important. His family engaged in times of prayer and singing. The other man was an agnostic. Not only did he not believe in God, he made fun of his neighbors. He railed at them when they were on their way to service, since he was in the field working. He even decided on the irrational plan of only working his crop when the neighbors were at church services, which involved every Sunday and midweek services. The Christian neighbor continued to take the derision and ridicule, and told his children that it really did not matter what their neighbor did. They still were going to believe in God. But one day, when accosted by his agnostic neighbor about do you think God is blessing you—can't you see he is blessing me more, the Christian replied, "God's final harvest is not in October."

It would do us well to remember that great truth—that there is a time of reckoning later on and it is not always here on this earth in material things. David had the right idea when he wrote, by inspiration, "The Lord will laugh at him; for he seeth that his day is coming" (v. 13).

When we worry and fret about evildoers and their deeds, it only upsets us. We continue to need to cling to the truth that God is blessing us. Do you remember the words that you learned in high school English, written by John Greenleaf Whittier, entitled "The Eternal Goodness?" Part of that poem says,

> Yet in the maddening maze of things,
> And tossed by storm and flood,
> To one fixed trust, my spirit clings;
> I know that God is good.

Trust in God

The Psalmist uses a number of interesting phrases that have to do with this secret of living forever. He says, "*Trust* in the Lord, and do good. Dwell in the land and feed on His faithfulness. *Delight* thyself also in Jehovah; He will give thee desire of thy heart. *Commit* thy ways unto Jehovah; *trust* also in Him and He will bring it to pass."

When we look at the list of positive things that David has to say about our relationship with the Lord it is rather impressive. We can trust in God with a faith that is unwavering, as was exemplified by Abraham. He went out not knowing where he was going, how long he would be gone, or where he would ultimately dwell. But he went in faith because he believed what God had said. We can live in delight by having daily communion with the Lord in prayer and meditation, and we can know that he is there in every way to help us.

When I think of commitment, I remember the story of the exhibitionist who pushed a wheelbarrow over Niagara Falls. After he had crossed over, he asked the crowd how many believed that he could cross blindfolded while pushing the wheelbarrow. Many hands went up. Then he asked, "Who would be willing to get in the wheelbarrow and ride across?" No one volunteered. The basic reason was that no one was committed to go with him under those circumstances.

Sometimes our biggest problem is that we just do not have time to "wait for the Lord" because of our impatience. We want things to go our way and for us to finish whatever we are doing now. Perhaps David's statement about waiting patiently for God is intended to help us to see that his ways and plans are not always ours. Isaiah also spoke of this waiting, in these words, "but they that wait for Jehovah shall renew their strength; they shall mount up with wings as eagles; they shall run, and not be weary; they shall walk, and not faint" (Isa. 40:31).

We find peace and happiness when we seek to honor God. In this sense, we are being meek. David says, "But the meek shall inherit the land" (v. 11). Many years later, Jesus repeated these same words in the Sermon on the Mount. The idea of meekness is really strength under control. The meekest man on the face of the earth was Moses. Yet, his example is one of intense strength and power, but it was always brought under control. He was able to be angry, without sinning.

When we have God as our helper, we will not be forsaken here. David's own experience has been the experience of many of us. From the very depth's of his heart, he wrote, "I have been young, and now am old; yet have I not seen the righteous forsaken, nor his seed begging bread" (v. 25). God does take care of his own. His providence is always there.

When we live on this earth in preparation for eternity, we need some examples to help guide us. David says, "Mark the perfect man . . . for there is a happy end to the man of peace" (v. 37). In view of a vast eternity, be at peace with yourself and your fellowman, obey God and serve him faithfully. Then you will be able to enjoy living forever. Our Lord promised that he was preparing a place for us. A place with room enough and to spare for all of those who are saved. It certainly behooves us to live here in preparation for that eternal home.

11. Thirsting

"As the hart panteth after the water-brooks, so panteth my soul after Thee, O God."

PSALM 42:1

Clovis Chappell told the following story in one of his books. "Years ago, as a lad, I was working one day in a field on the back side of my father's farm. This field was washed by the songful waters of the Buffalo River. Away in the distance on the opposite side of the farm stood a range of rugged and majestic hills. Suddenly, from among these hills I heard the baying of a pack of hounds. My attention was all the more alert because, we ourselves did not keep hounds. As I listened, the baying became more and more distinct. By this I knew that the pack was coming toward me. Then as I waited in expectation, I was startled to see a deer suddenly come into view. The pursuing hounds were dreadfully upon its heels. It was easy to see the poor creature was almost spent. But on he came, running desperately for his life. Then as he saw me in his path, in an effort to turn, he dropped to his knees. Immediately the hounds had their cruel fangs at his throat, and the long chase was over.

"Why was this deer running in my direction? It was not that he expected any help of my hands. He was as fearful of me as of the hounds that hung upon his heels. He was running toward me because he was making for the river that lay just behind me. That brook offered everything to this poor spent creature. It offered escape from the deadly foes that were thirsting for his blood. It offered rest for his body that was wearied by long hours of desperate running. It offered satisfaction for his burning thirst. It offered life, itself. 'If I can only reach this brook,' he might have said to himself, 'I shall live. I shall again have an opportunity to realize my destiny in the glad freedom of my native hills.' No wonder this poor pursued hart was panting for the water brook."

This is the picture of the Psalmist. His is a soul in trouble, and he feels cast down. Others are beginning to mock and ask him about "his God."

He pours out his very soul in these words, "My soul thirsteth for God, for the living God: when shall I come and appear before God? My tears have been my food, day and night, while they continue to say unto me, Where is thy God?" (vv. 2, 3). A hint into the meaning of the 42nd Psalm is the superscription found in some Bibles, "Thirsting for God in Trouble and Exile."

The Great Yearning

The author of this brief cry, has been running even as a deer, panting for breath. His thirst is real. He thirsts for the living God. He is tired of the taunts of his enemies, and tired of existing on tears for days on end, and now he turns to seek God.

This man's experience was not unique, but represents the universal craving and thirst of all mankind.

Many years later, Jesus said in his famous "Sermon on the Mount," in the section we call the Beatitudes, "Blessed are those who hunger and thirst after righteousness, for they shall be filled" (Matt. 5:6). Every soul knows this thirsting and longing. And the only way it can be satisfied, is to turn to God.

We remember the example of the prodigal son, whose thoughts turned homeward when he was at the lowest ebb of his life. It was the memory of home and father that caused him to start his journey back. The husks that the swine did eat were not food for his soul.

An unnamed woman at Jacob's well in Sychar came to Jesus one day by accident. Though she came to draw water from the well, her needs were far more than for well water. Her needs were so deep that the only thing that could satisfy her was "living water."

Jesus told the story of the rich fool who thought he had everything, and had laid up much goods for many years. Yet, his soul was not satisfied. He did not have what was really the most needful. That very night he had to give account of himself, because he came to the end of life.

The Psalmist remembers back to happy days, when he worshipped in the house of God, singing with joy and praise. He even remembers the land around the Jordan River, and the hills that stretch in the background. But now he is bowed down in sorrow and anxiety and grief. He is soul-sick.

Isaiah seemed to know of this great yearning, for he issued the invitation, "lo, everyone that thirsteth, come ye to the waters" (Isa. 55:1). The last invitation in the Bible speaks again of this desire of the soul and our great thirst by saying, ". . . and he that is athirst, let him come; he that will, let him take the water of life freely" (Rev. 22:17).

> I heard the voice of Jesus say, Behold I freely give.
> The living water; thirsty one, stoop down and drink and live.
> I came to Jesus and I drank of that life-giving stream;
> My thirst was quenched, my soul revived, and now I live in Him.

The Feeling of Loneliness

Twice in this Psalm, and continued in the next one, the Psalmist cries out, "Why art thou cast down, O my soul? Why art thou disquieted within me?" (vv. 5, 11; 43:5).

Here is a man speaking to his soul, as we often say in conversation, "So I said to myself." But in many ways this is an upsetting voice of a troubled lonely soul in anguish.

All of us know the times of being cast down. Most of the time we refer to it as the "blues." Our mood changes. Our spirit goes down; we feel very low. Sometimes it's the weather on a bitter gray day in which we feel that we have little reason for living. It could be our own feelings, for when we ache in body or mind, we are really not ourselves. Sometimes it's due to worry when there is illness of someone we love, or perhaps it is fear and uncertainty of the tomorrows. We can even be dispirited when we have heavy decisions to make.

Longfellow was right when he wrote the lines, "Into each life some rain must fall. Some days must be dark and dreary."

Elijah, one of God's courageous prophets, felt the blues on one occasion. After the great contest at Mt. Carmel, he hid in a cave, scared out of his wits by the threat of Queen Jezebel. He even prayed to God and told him that he was ready to die, that life was not worth living.

But loneliness and the blues is never the final answer. Like the tides of the great ocean, they go out, but they come back in. Even the Psalmist recognized this. The last word was not hopelessness but rather hope.

"Hope thou in God; for I shall yet praise him, who is the help of my countenance and my God." The night is never too dark, nor the day too long that we cannot look up and by faith see God. Our hope can go on and on, believing, trusting, and waiting.

Who has not been inspired by these moving words of Alice Hawthorne, which describes the beauty of hope:

> Soft as the voice of an angel,
> Breathing a lesson unheard,
> Hope with a gentle persuasion
> Whispers her comforting word;

Wait till the darkness is over,
Wait till the tempest is done,
Hope for the sunshine tomorrow,
After the showers are gone.

12. Refuge

"God is our refuge and strength, A very present help in trouble."

PSALM 46:1

Martin Luther especially loved the 46th Psalm. In his own life, there were times when he was cast down in spirit. It was then that the great reformer would say to his companion, Melanchthon, "Come, Philip, let us sing the 46th Psalm." Luther's hymn, "A Mighty Fortress" is based on this Psalm. We still sing the words of his majestic hymn!

A mighty fortress is our God,
A bulwark never failing:
Our Helper He, amid the flood
Of mortal ills prevailing.

Twice in the Psalm is the refrain, "Jehovah of hosts is with us; The God of Jacob is our refuge" (vv. 7, 11). This is really the theme of the Psalm. As understood by the Psalmist, all those who dwell in Zion will have refuge in God. Yet for us the meaning is that God does care and protect us. He is the Christian's refuge. All of us go to him for our strength in our own times of trouble.

The Averted Battle

Many Bible students think that the situation behind the writing of the 46th Psalm is the miraculous deliverance of Jerusalem from the army of Sennacherib. King Hezekiah placed his hope and dependance upon God, but from human eyes, the situation seemed hopeless. The only assurance Hezekiah had been given was from Isaiah, the prophet.

The hosts of Assyria were mighty, powerful and organized. They had already defeated many other nations, and the gods of these people had not been able to save them. Yet on the night before the battle, the angel of the Lord went forth and killed 185,000 of the Assyrians. Jerusalem was saved! Hezekiah's faith was justified.

Since "God is our refuge and strength, a very present help in trouble," the Psalmist declares, "therefore will we not fear, though the earth do change, and though the mountains be shaken into the heart of the seas: though the waters thereof roar and be troubled, though the mountains tremble with the swelling thereof." The people *knew this* and rejoiced.

The impressive thing to our minds is that God is there when we need him. He is not somewhere over the rainbow, but here, right *now*.

There Is a River

Suddenly the Psalmist changes. Our God is not only a Protector, but he is also a Provider. After the thunder, "there is a river." The picture of the gently flowing river, with all its streams refreshing the land, is a symbol of God's presence. Such a source of life-giving water makes glad the citizens of the city of God. This is because it is *living water*.

The reason for such confidence is that "God is in the midst of her." Whatever our condition, God knows. If we feel beseiged, he is there with us. If we are burdened with a pressing problem, he understands. If we must walk through the dark valley of sorrow, he goes with us. When we are his saints, he will not let anyone trifle with us. We shall not be moved.

I especially appreciate the line, "God will help her, and that right early." The original language suggests, as the footnote indicates, that God will help us at the first light of day. He is there at the earliest hour to share our problems and woes. He does not forget us or forsake us. We have all heard that the darkest hour comes before the dawn, but we have the confidence that God will be there to meet us.

Other peoples resent the security of God's people. Therefore, they rage against us. Even when the evil forces of a Sennacherib attack us, God is still in control. When he utters his voice, the foes melt before him.

Be Still and Know

The people of Jerusalem, just like faithful Christians today, are invited to see the works of God. What he accomplishes is amazing. He destroys the destroyer. He is in this world to win, not just a battle, but totally until "the last enemy" is destroyed. He still can break the bow, and cut the spear and burn the chariot.

Instead of our being so concerned about the enemy and the forces of this world, the Psalmist pleads with us for the Lord, "Be still and know that I am God." All of us need to stop—meditate—pause in the midst of busy and frustrated living and realize that we have a *Power* greater than anything the world knows. Our problem is that often we are trying to do God's work, but instead we can relax and let God work.

I know a lady, Zita Smith, who every day reads aloud this particular Psalm. For her, and countless others, it brings strength and help. I believe the reason is that all of us need to have the assurance that God is our refuge, that "Jehovah of hosts is with us," that the same God who watched over Jacob is still watching us.

> Other refuge have I none,
> Hangs my helpless soul on Thee;
> Leave, O leave me not alone,
> Still support and comfort me.

13. Sin

> "For I know my transgressions, and my sin is ever before me. Against thee, thee only, have I sinned."
>
> PSALM 51:3-4

One of the first sermons that I ever tried to preach was based on David's prayer in Psalm 51. I think the intriguing thing about this particular Psalm is that it is the confession of David after his terrible sin. How could a good man like David, so loved by both his people and the Lord, commit such a sin! Then, God forgave him and loved him again. And in our minds there is the question, "Can this happen to us also?" There is nothing more powerful than this confession and restitution.

How the Sin Overcame Him

David had succeeded; he felt that he had arrived. He no longer was trying to establish himself as a leader of men; he was the King. Because of this, he was in his most dangerous position due to his success. He had also reached the period of middle life. It has been observed that the 40's can be the most dangerous time in life for men and women. It's a time of reflection, looking backward over the things that have been accomplished, and maybe even of things dreamed of as yet unfulfilled. It's also a time of looking forward and realizing that life is going rapidly, and something needs to be done.

David was idle. He had reached the time in his life when he felt he had nothing in particular to do after living a busy life. The Bible specifically states that it was the time of the year when Kings go forth to battle, but David remained behind (2 Sam. 11:1). Nature abhors a vacuum.

His sin started only as a thought, an innocent look, but it grew into an act. The lustful sin committed with Bathsheba was in the heat of passion, and is not to be compared with the cold-blooded murder of a loyal, faithful servant, Uriah. David became a homewrecker and a murderer, but he never dreamed in his wildest imagination that his sin would go this far. This man, who was a man after God's own heart, broke five of the Ten Commandments.

All of the facts of the story are well known to us, and the Bible does not try to get around them in any sense, but tells the truth. But, what we are interested in is David's way back to divine favor. First, God sent him a preacher, Nathan. He called what David had done *sin*. Then David, as king, did a most unusual thing, he wept in bitter repentance. He poured out his soul in prayer. It was truly a sinner's prayer. David becomes one of the few men in all of Scripture who said, "I have sinned."

Listen to his earnest prayer:

> Have mercy upon me, O God, according to thy lovingkindness; according unto the multitude of thy tender mercies, blot out my transgressions.
>
> Wash me thoroughly from my iniquity, and cleanse me from my sin. For I acknowledge my transgressions: and my sin is ever before me. Against thee, thee only, have I sinned, and done this evil in thy sight: that thou mightest be justified when thou speakest, and be clear when thou judgest. . . .
>
> Purify me with hyssop, and I shall be clean: wash me, and I shall be whiter than snow.
>
> Make me to hear joy and gladness: that the bones which thou hast broken may rejoice.

Hide thy face from my sins, and blot out all mine iniquities.

Create in me a clean heart, O God; and renew a right spirit within me.

Cast me not away from thy presence; and take not thy holy spirit from me.

Restore unto me the joy of thy salvation; and uphold me with a free spirit.

(Ps. 51:1-4, 7-12)

Prayer for Forgiveness and Cleansing

David admits his sin. This is the first step for all of us in getting right with God. We can't help but notice the personality that comes through with David admitting, "*I* have sinned," "*my* sin," "*my* iniquity," and "*my* transgression." He offers no excuse or mitigating circumstances. How often we, as individuals, confess others' faults but never our own. Or, we may confess great sins but lay the blame at the door of someone else. David learned that all rebellion is against God. And the one that is hurt the most is God, himself. Of course, sin hurts other people, but it is our divine parent that is most grieved.

David made his request for mercy. After his confession, he knew he still needed the love and mercy of God. It is favor beyond what is deserved. Notice that David does not pray for mercy according to his sincerity, or his rank and position, or even his genius, but according to God's lovingkindness. It is a prayer for infinite mercy, and that is what we need today. "According to the mercy, the multitude of thy tender mercies blot out my transgressions."

Then David goes on to tell of the content of that mercy. He wants to be washed clean, completely. Notice the triple nature of sin as used by David. Transgression, meaning "defection from God," iniquity meaning "perversion of right, deprivity of conduct," and sin meaning "missing the mark in life or wandering from the right way." Yet, as bad as the sin is, David wants to be completely clean and whole again.

Also, we note that there is the triple removing of guilt. David asked that his sin be blotted out as a debt in God's book that needs to be erased, to be washed as one would wash clothes, and to be cleansed, meaning after being washed being pronounced clean, even as a leper has been cured.

Next, David asked for a new heart, or a new nature. This refers to the inner man, or the attitude that we have. He wants desperately to have the right spirit within him. David is concerned lest when he comes back that he will not feel the same closeness and intimacy with God; so he sincerely prays that he not be cast away, but rather that God will "restore unto me the joy of thy salvation." It is easy for us to feel that we have lost closeness with God, and so all of us need to pray this same prayer.

If God will do these things for him, David promises to go and tell sinners of their evil ways and to bring them back to the right paths. It is the same as saying that he is a converted sinner, more impressed than ever with the ways and wonders of God. He now has a message to tell others, and he will do it effectively. Each of us must come to the point where we can go and tell what God has done for us.

What were the results of this prayer? God heard it and saved him. The sinner rises from his knees, and he is a better man. If God heard David, he will hear me. Does not this bring courage and strength to your heart? All it takes is the willingness to make a confession of sin, knowing that God will hear and cleanse.

Lord Jesus, I long to be perfectly whole;
I want Thee forever to live in my soul;
Break down every idol, cast out every foe:
Now wash me, and I shall be whiter than snow.

14. Forgiveness

"Blessed is he whose transgression is forgiven, whose sin is covered."
PSALM 32:1

Is there some experience in your life that makes you feel guilty? Perhaps it was when you were a youth, and you slipped and did something against your parents' wishes, or it may have been later in life, that you made some mistake in dealing with the wrong person, some night of horror now in your mind. It could be your inner secret alone, but it has troubled and bothered you ever since.

There is no one that knew more remorse and guilt for the twin sins of adultery and murder than David. Yet, he experienced the blessing of forgiveness. As Psalm 51 was written as his prayer, asking for forgiveness, so Psalm 32 was written after he knew the forgiveness of God. It could well be that it is the message that you need most.

Pardon and Cleansing

What wonderful assurance! "Blessed is he whose sin is forgiven," because it is completely covered. Here is a jubilant cry of relief; David is rejoicing! The Jews used this particular Psalm on the Day of Atonement to describe the Lord's forgiveness of sins. So annually, the ancient people called to mind again the words of David and expressed their own relief at the forgiveness of their sins by using his words.

When God forgives, he forgets. Thus, nothing can

stand between us and him. The Psalmist says, "Blessed is the man unto whom Jehovah imputeth not iniquity, and in whose spirit there is no guile." God is willing to remove all the stain and guilt of sin. It is a complete cleansing.

But this is not to say, that David does not see the awfulness of sin. He does, for he has experienced it. He calls sin transgression, which means "separation or departure from God." It can lead to rebellion, and in his case did. He also calls sin "a missing of the mark," like shooting an arrow and never hitting the bullseye. Sin is always a blunder in the eyes of God on man's part. Further, David labeled sin iniquity, meaning "something twisted or distorted." It is like a wavering, crooked line, that we sometimes see in the middle of a street when the person making the line goes astray.

In David's own words, he writes, "I acknowledge my sin to thee, and mine iniquity did I not hide: I said, I will confess my transgression unto Jehovah; and thou forgavest the iniquity of my sin."

Yet God's forgiveness is as great as the sin. It is as though he removes a great burden, a heavy hand that had been placed on David. One of the most beautiful stories I know coming out of World War II is the story of Jacob Deshaver and Captain Cato. Captain Cato, a Japanese official, had Jacob Deshaver in a concentration camp. He was mean and rough to all the men under him, and tried to break their spirit. The torture was so intense that Jacob Deshaver resolved in his mind that one day he would get even with this terrible man.

But in the turn of events, Jacob Deshaver, after coming back home, was converted and decided to preach the story of Christ. He resolved to return to Japan and preach to these people, who had been his enemies. One night while preaching, he was startled when Captain Cato came in response to the plea to follow Jesus. How could Jacob Deshaver even think of reaching out and shaking hands with his former tormenter? Yet he thought of the love and forgiveness of Jesus, and was able to bring himself to do just this. When he forgave him and accepted him as a brother, he learned how sweet forgiveness can really be.

God cleanses our inward pollution and filthiness. At first, David had tried to bury his sin, and it was then that he was most miserable. The night seemed longer because his burden of sin was so heavy. In the daytime he could not get his thoughts on other things, due to the overriding problem that harrassed him. He suffered mental and physical anguish. But now, God has removed the sin as though it were a debt that was charged against him. God says, in effect, "Not guilty!"

Confessing Sin for Salvation

The reason the Psalmist knew such blessedness is that he confessed his sin to God. He first had to acknowledge the sin and forgive himself. Then he had to tell God of his feelings. He did this effectively, as we have already seen in the 51st Psalm. If we ever learn the blessing of forgiveness, we must learn the principal of confessing our sins. The New Testament teaches, "Confess therefore your sins one to another, and pray one for another, that ye may be healed. The supplication of a righteous man availeth much in its working" (James 5:16).

It is possible for us to be as stubborn as a mule in regard to forgiveness and confession. David writes, "Be ye not as the horse, or as the mule, which have no understanding." There are some people who just wouldn't admit fault or sin if their life depended on it. These are the people who just cannot understand that they are hurting themselves more than anyone else. David is right, "many sorrows shall be to the wicked."

Charles Allen tells the story of a woman in a small town in Alabama who was forced to run a lumber yard, after the death of her husband. Since she did not know much about the business, she relied heavily on her foreman. However, after several months, he went to work for her competitor. Her heart was filled with hatred, and then she asked the question, "Why did he do this to me? Did he not realize that I am a widow and was depending on his help?" One night in a church service, she heard a message from Dr. Allen concerning Jesus' death on the cross. He especially emphasized the prayer of Christ from the cross that was for his enemies. He asked that the entire audience listen as it were to hear the words again, "Father, forgive them, for they know not what they do." It was like an echo reaching into the very heart of this troubled woman. Tears began to course down her cheeks, as the malice and hatred began to leave her heart. She had to learn to forgive even this foreman that she considered her enemy.

Only when we learn to pray for our enemies and to forgive them can we know the joy and happiness of forgiveness. The only true joy comes from trusting in the Lord. David recognized the blessing of being right in God's eyes, and it is then that we can shout for joy. David closes the Psalm by saying, "Be glad in Jehovah, and rejoice, ye righteous; and shout for joy, all ye that are upright in heart."

When Dr. Christian Bernard first made a heart transplant, it was sensational, world-wide news. Even after several heart transplants were done, it was still considered something novel and unusual. Yet, this was David's plea in the long ago, "Create in me a clean heart, O God." This should be our desire, too. But the only way that we can have a new heart is to be in Christ. He is willing to remove all of our sins, and make us *new creatures*. "Draw near with a true heart in fullness of faith, having our hearts sprinkled from an evil conscience, and having our bodies washed in pure water" (Heb. 10:22).

15. Burdens

"Cast thy burden upon Jehovah, and he will sustain you: He will never suffer the righteous to be moved."
PSALM 55:22

Look at our average day. We leap out of bed fifteen minutes late, gulp down our coffee, bolt down our food, whiz into town, darting from lane to lane, dash for the office, rattle off some letters, rush to lunch, tear out for home, and drop dead.

How often we say, "I'm so frustrated, I'm so worried. My soul is cracked with care." This seems to be true with the whole world, for we are overwhelmed with problems, sorrows, and troubles. The writer of the 55th Psalm was a burdened man, but I believe that he came to the right conclusion in regard to his burdens—that he is to cast his burden upon the Lord.

What Do We Do With Our Burdens?

It's a truism that all of us have burdens to bear. You know the old spiritual that says, "Nobody knows the troubles I've seen, nobody knows but Jesus." Even Job, the great patriarch who was tested and proved his patience, once said, "Man that is born of a woman, is of few days, and full of trouble" (Job 14:1). So to have a burden or problem is not a unique thing, but how we handle it. What do we do with our burdens?

First, we are not to doubt God. He is ever near us, and does care for our welfare. The apostle Peter in a remarkable statement said, "cast(ing) all thine anxiety on him, for he careth for you" (1 Peter 5:7).

Our first line of defense must be to go to him, and rely on his promise that he will not place on us more than we can bear. The Psalmist begins at the right place, by saying, "Give ear to my prayers, O God; and hide not thyself from my supplication."

Second, we must not engage in complaining or indulge in self-pity. The Psalmist could have gone this route. He even said, "I am restless in my complaint, and moan, because of the voice of the enemy, because of the oppression of the wicked; for they cast iniquity upon me and in anger they persecute me. My heart is sore pained within me: and the terrors of death are fallen upon me. Fearfulness and trembling are come upon me, and horror hath overwhelmed me." One of the most impressive stories is of how Hellen Keller, the deaf, blind girl became an effective teacher and personality due to the influence of her teacher, also legally blind, Annie Sullivan. These two ladies worked together and were a great inspiration to the entire world, but they were too busy to ever engage in self-pity. People who go this route always end up the loser.

Third, we must not yield to the desire to escape. Even this thought crossed the Psalmist's mind. He uttered a truth when he said, "Oh that I had the wings like a dove! Then would I fly away and be at rest. Lo, then would I wander far off. I would lodge in the wilderness." You remember the old story of Br'er Rabbit in the Uncle Remus Tales. Br'er Rabbit was so filled with trouble that he just decided to leave home and never come back, but after he was gone for just a little while, he returned home because he learned that troubles can be anywhere. Most of us, if we could see all the troubles of the world hung out on a vast clothesline, would not exchange our troubles for somebody else's. It is just best not to try to escape or to "fly away."

Fourth, we must not become embittered against others. Here we have one of the saddest things that can happen to a person as the Psalmist writes, "But it was thou, a man mine equal, my companion, and my familiar friend. We took sweet counsel together; we walked in the house of God with the throng." Some Bible students think that this refers to the rebellion in David's own household, led by his son, Absalom. Certainly, this was a dark day in the history of David. It looked as though he would lose not only the throne, the capital city of Jerusalem, but even his life was threatened. To think that the enemy was his own son.

I also believe that these words are written prophetically of Christ and the experience that happened to him in being sold out by Judas Iscariot. Yet, the companion, the supposed friend, was willing to cooperate with the enemy to get rid of the Lord. But Jesus did not become embittered toward Judas but rather felt sorry for him. It was Abraham Lincoln who said that the best way to get rid of enemies was to make them friends. Stephen, while being stoned to death, died with a prayer on his lips for his enemies. The answer to our question, finally must be, to call upon God for help. This is exactly what the Psalmist did. He wrote, "As for me, I will call upon God, and Jehovah will save me." God not only knows our problems, but he is able to sustain us and take care of us in a time of need. He knows and understands. The old hymn says,

> Cast thy burden on the Lord,
> Only lean upon his words;
> Thou shalt soon have cause to bless
> His eternal faithfulness.

The Lord Promises to Help Us

Often it is best for us to accept the fact that the burdens we have are given to us as a means of testing. The word burden as it is used in verse 22 of this Psalm can mean, "that which he hath given thee," according to the footnote. If this is the case, it simply means that the Lord is testing us by means of some problem or situation, and when we respond in the way that we should, it will be a means of drawing us closer to the Lord and to those we love.

Yet, let us not forget that he says unto us, "cast thy burden upon Jehovah." Cast means to "fling or hurl" and denotes action and effort. The Bible says that Daniel was "cast" into the lion's den, Jonah was "cast" into the sea, and John the Baptist was "cast" into prison. This means to just fling it down and leave it there.

When we cast our burdens on the Lord, we are recognizing the fact that he is the great Burden Bearer. Even in his great invitation Jesus announced, "Come unto me all ye that labor and are heavy laden, and I will give you rest. Take my yoke upon you, and learn of me, for I am meek and lowly in heart and ye shall find rest unto your soul, for my yoke is easy and my burden is light" (Matt. 11:28-30). We may not be able to bear these heavy loads, but we know one who can.

The example of the apostle Paul in his affliction comes readily to mind. Paul told us that he had a thorn in the flesh, and he did not know what to do about it. Three times he called upon the Lord to remove this affliction. Finally, he received an answer that sustained him. The Lord's word was, "My grace is sufficient for thee; for my power is made perfect in weakness." With this understanding in mind, Paul could say, "Most gladly, therefore, will I rather glory in my weaknesses, that the power of Christ may rest upon me" (2 Cor. 12:9).

BURDENS

When you have cast your burden down at the feet of the Lord, leave it there. Don't take it to him and then pick it back up. He will assume full responsibility for the burden and for you. His promise is that he will sustain and uphold us. He will never suffer the righteous to be moved.

16. Wicked

"For I was envious at the foolish, when I saw the prosperity of the wicked."

PSALM 73:3

Have you ever felt like you tried to do good and be righteous, only to fail or even to fall? At the same time, have you looked at those who were worldly and unrighteous and saw that they were succeeding? If so, this powerful 73rd Psalm has a message for you. It is the spiritual biography of a man who confesses that his feet "were almost gone" and that his steps "had well nigh slipped." Your experience may be like his, in that you had slipped and were down, maybe even fallen prostrate.

The Prosperity of the Wicked

The Psalmist's problem was that the wicked prospered and the righteous seemed to be perishing. He first observed their prosperity, as evidenced by the fact that their health was good, they were free from any trouble, and they had all that their heart could desire. He said that even their eyes stood out with fatness. No wonder they scoffed at God and his people.

When the Psalmist realized all of this, it was more than he could take. It simply wasn't fair. He could well have uttered the familiar words of an old song,

> When death has come and taken our loved ones,
> It leaves our home so lonely and drear;

Then do we wonder while others prosper,
Living so wicked, year after year.

This was not a new problem, and it remains with us, even today. Bildad, the Shuhite, one of Job's friends, accused him of being wicked, and even perhaps secretive in this wickedness, as the reason for his suffering. Bildad said, "If thou wert pure and upright: surely now He would awake for thee, and make the habitation of thy righteousness prosper" (Job 8:6).

We need to learn that prosperity is not a sure sign of the smile of God, and neither is adversity an indication of his displeasure and indignation. It was this kind of thought that had led the Psalmist to nearly slip. His cry was,

Behold, these are the wicked;
And, being always at ease,
They increase in riches.
Surely in vain have I cleansed my heart,
And washed my hands in innocency;
For all the day long have I been plagued,
And chastened every morning.
If I had said, "I will speak thus;
Behold, I had dealt treacherously with the generation of thy children."

He is distressed and upset. It is just not fair to him to see wicked people living in luxury. How can they have more and do more and be content, when they have lived lives that are displeasing to God. Why is it that the righteous seem to suffer, have less, and make sacrifices?

Yet, the Psalmist makes a statement that lets us know he has changed. He is now able to believe in the goodness of God. Verse 1 of this Psalm is really his conclusion. He says, "Surely God is good to Israel, even to such as are pure in heart." What happened?

The Steadying Influence

The Psalmist thought on his ways, and up to this point, he had been relying on human reasoning. Then he went to spiritual thinking. The big change in his life and attitude was brought about by this right kind of thinking.

He said, "When I thought how I might know this, it was too painful for me; until I went into the sanctuary of God, and considered their latter end. Surely thou settest them in slippery places: thou castest them down into destruction."

He had time to reflect when he went into the sanctuary of God. His thinking was altered. Life, in its true focus, came into view. He needed time to get himself allied with the godly people and squared with God. His whole thought had been, "Things are going badly with me and well with the ungodly."

This type of thinking is the kind that says today, "Jesus was only a man who was born in a stable, lived, ate, and drank like all other men, did his work as a carpenter, and was crucified in utter weakness on a cross." If these are the facts, why am I to believe that he is the son of God? It is impossible. Matthew Arnold once said, "Miracles cannot happen, therefore miracles haven't happened." This is another indication of the wrong kind of thinking.

All of us realize that before a man or woman can become a Christian, he must give up this kind of thinking. The Christian must come as a believer in God and in his son. By faith, we accept all that the New Testament says about his son and his vicarious death for our sins. But, what so often happens is that this wrong kind of thinking influences us after we become a Christian, also.

Our thinking must be changed from rational to spiritual. Isaiah wrote these words for God, "For my thoughts are not your thoughts, neither are your ways my ways, saith Jehovah" (Isa. 55:8). The thinking of the Psalmist was changed as he went to worship. It was here that he thought of his fellow worshippers and stopped thinking just of himself. You also will begin to experience that others may have deeper troubles than you have had, but many of them also radiate joy and peace and confidence. Then you start thinking of the whole history of how God has dealt with his people, protecting them and caring for them.

He further realized that their latter end was not good at all, for they are to be destroyed. All of us must ultimately take the long view and look at where the wicked are headed, in contrast to where the righteous are headed. Jesus urged his followers, "Enter ye in by the narrow gate: for wide is the gate, and broad is the way, that leadeth to destruction, and many are they that enter in thereby. For narrow is the gate, and straightened the way, that leadeth unto life, and few are they that find it" (Matt. 7:13-14).

The Latter End

This is what matters. Where are the wicked headed? Charles Darwin confessed at the end of his life that as a result of concentrating on one aspect of life, he lost the power to enjoy poetry and music. H. G. Wells is another who ridiculed Christianity while claiming so much for the mind and human understanding. But Wells was baffled and bewildered at the end of his life, and wrote a book entitled, *Mind at the End of Its Tether*.

In contrast to the wicked's end, there are the encouraging valedictory words of the apostle Paul. Here is how a good man can come to the end of a journey. "The time of my departure is come. I have fought the good fight, I have finished the course, I have kept the faith: henceforth there is laid up for me the crown of righteousness, which the Lord, the righteous judge, shall give to me at that day" (2 Tim. 4:6-8).

Perhaps the simplest comment is one that the Psalmist uttered in the opening Psalm of the book. He said, "The wicked are not so, but are like the chaff which the wind driveth away." The wicked do not stand.

17. Righteous

"Whom have I in heaven but thee? And there is none upon earth that I desire besides thee."

PSALM 73:25

Let us take another look at a man of centuries ago who had a problem so similar to our own day. The author of the 73rd Psalm thought that the wicked were prospering, while he was slipping and falling. The basic problem was that his thinking was wrong. He was thinking rationally, as a human being, rather than as a spiritual person, with thoughts that see the whole picture. In fact, his thinking was wrong in three respects.

Wrong Thinking About the Ungodly

He had been unfair in his estimation of how much pleasure and prosperity the wicked had and how lacking he was in these respects. What he at first saw was on the surface, but on mature reflection he found that they were the ones who were really on slippery ground. It is easy for us to make the contrast with the wicked's prosperity and our seeming lack of it, but be unfair with the facts. Have we forgotten, too, about the destruction of the flood, about the fire that came down from heaven and destroyed Sodom and Gomorrah, about the Philistines, with their great leader Goliath, or about the Assyrians and Babylonians? But the greatest triumph of all over the devil and the forces of wickedness, is the resurrection of Jesus Christ. Our Lord said, "I will build my church, and the gates of Hades shall not prevail against it" (Matt. 16:18). Jesus announced to his apostles and to the world that there would be no Hadean force, not even death itself, that would keep him from accomplishing his purpose which was to build a kingdom of righteousness.

Not only are the wicked miserable here on earth, they are afraid of the future. Their end is destruction. Many people quote the poem of William Henley, called "Invictus," as a means of citing courage. Yet the man who wrote these very words, himself, committed suicide. He also said of the future, "Beyond this place of wrath and tears looms but the horror of the shade." With these thoughts in mind, now read the poem.

> Out of the night that covers me,
> Black as the pit, from pole to pole,
> I thank whatever gods may be,
> For my unconquerable soul.
>
> In the fell clutch of circumstance,
> I have not winced nor cried aloud,
> Under the bludgeoning of chance
> My head is bloody but unbowed.
>
> Beyond this place of wrath and tears
> Looms but the horror of the shade,
> And yet the menace of the years,
> Finds and shall find me unafraid.
>
> It matters not how straight the gate,
> How charged with punishment the scroll;
> I am the master of my fate,
> I am the captain of my soul.

The thought of the kind of punishment that the wicked receive is enough to cause us to stop and think. We need to remember that the wicked are cast into outer darkness, where there is weeping and gnashing of teeth. Hell is described as a place where the fire burneth forever (Matt. 25:30; Mark 9:43).

The Psalmist finally learned to think correctly, for in his own words he said, "Until I went into the sanctuary of God, and considered their latter end. Surely thou settest them in slippery places: thou castest them down to destruction" (v. 17-18).

Wrong Thinking About Himself

But the Psalmist also had wrong thinking about himself. In his own confusion and feelings of hurt and pride, he decided to just give up. Life wasn't worth it. This kind of thinking can lead any of us astray, and we rationalize ourselves into thinking that it really doesn't matter, for no one cares anyway.

The Psalmist really rethought himself. He said, "For my soul was grieved, and I was pricked in my heart: so broodish was I, and ignorant; I was as a beast before thee," (vv. 21-22). This led him to a confession. He calls himself "stupid as a beast." Our expression today, "stubborn as a mule," carries the same idea.

Can we not say, "God, I am a sinner." Do we bring our confession to him? Even as Christians, we have to keep being renewed, rededicated to God. Perhaps, Paul would be our ideal of one of the greatest Christians whoever lived. But even Paul said, "But I buffet my body, and bring it into bondage: lest by any means, after that I have preached to others, I myself should be rejected" (1 Cor. 9:27). The Psalmist's real problem was himself. His heart was wrong, his thinking was out of kilter. Things only began to be right when he realized again his need and dependance upon God, and he cried out, "Whom have I in Heaven but thee; there is none upon earth that I desire besides thee" (v. 25).

God was still there to help and guide him, even as he is still there for you. It is only with this realization that we can make it in this world. Perhaps we need to learn to say these words with the apostle Paul, "For I have learned, in whatsoever state I am, therein to be content. I know how to be abased, and I know also how to abound: in everything and in all things have I learned the secret both to be filled and to be hungry, both to abound and to be in want. I can do all things in him that strengtheneth me" (Phil. 4:11-13).

David wrote in an earlier Psalm, "Mark the perfect man, and behold the upright; for there is a happy end to the man of peace" (Ps. 37:37). It is still so.

Wrong Thinking About God

The Psalmist also had wrong thinking about God. This too was a mistake. Had God forsaken him? Has God forgotten us? Has he ceased to be gracious? He finally acknowledged, "Surely thou settest them in slippery places" (v. 18). God still controls the world.

He then added, "It is good for me to draw near to God" (v. 28). Where else is there to go? Peter acknowledged this truth to Christ. After a number of disciples had turned away, Jesus, thinking that his own chosen would also follow them, asked, "Will ye also go away?" Peter replied, "Lord, to whom shall we go, thou hast the words of eternal life" (John 6:67-69).

To try to answer the question about why God allows a sinner to prosper, think of these reasons. First, he permits it in order that sin may be revealed for what it is, to manifest itself in ugliness. Second, it can also be partly for the punishment of sin, since they reap the consequences of their own sin. Thirdly, he allows it to display his own greatness and glory over this mighty enemy. Fourth, it is sometimes used to punish the righteous as a means of discipline.

The Psalmist concludes that God is good to Israel and to all who are of a pure heart. His confidence is strong. Who else can he go to—whom can he turn? Only God. Now he is ready to go out and tell others of God. He has passed through the temptation of nearly slipping by losing his faith, but now all is secure.

> Thou the spring of all my comfort,
> More than life to me,
> Whom have I on earth beside thee?
> Whom in heaven but thee?

18. Worship

> "My soul longeth, yea, even fainteth for the courts of Jehovah."
>
> PSALM 84:2

Where would you rather be than anywhere else? Where is the loveliest spot on earth to you? For the Psalmist of the 84th Psalm, it was an easy answer. It was to be in the presence of the Lord in the temple of Jerusalem.

Granted, there is a difference in time and situation, but I think that high on our priority list should be the worship of the church. We want to be in the presence of the Lord.

The Delights of the Worshipper

For the Jew there was a special thrill in making a pilgrimage to Jerusalem to worship. As you are aware, they had songs that they sang along the way, recorded in Psalms 120-134. Often it was the trip of a lifetime, as they had carefully saved over the years for it. Often the sight of the holy city brought tears to the eyes, a thrill to the soul, and ecstasy to life. The Psalmist says he almost faints when he considers the privilege of being able to worship there.

He compares the blessing of being in the temple with a sparrow who builds her nest there, in verse 3. Would it not be wonderful if we had this feeling of wanting to be with the Lord and his people at the hours of worship and devotion? Those who are in the house of the Lord are given this blessing, "Blessed are they that dwell in the house: they will be still praising thee" (v. 4).

I remember Barbara Barker, the talented, creative lady, who used the idea from this Psalm in teaching children at Vacation Bible School. She made for each child a nest out of a half of a walnut shell, putting straw inside, and made a tiny bird out of the end of a pine cone. Each child was given this little nest with this scripture pasted to it about the sparrow building her nest in the house of the Lord, and the resulting blessing for us of praising God's name in his house. What an object lesson!

Another wonderful benefit of worship, is that even though we may go through the, "Valley of Weeping," we will be given strength by the Lord. God never fails us or forgets us. We will be able to go from strength to strength because of his presence.

Some time ago, I read of a man in Kansas City who was in an explosion. As a result of this disaster, he lost both his hands and his eyes. He wanted so much to be able to stay in touch with God that he learned to read the Bible with the use of his tongue. How marvelous that he was willing even in this way with the sense of touch to read God's Word.

Trust in the Lord

The whole reason behind the value of worship is our trusting the Lord: he makes the difference. One of my favorite verses in this Psalm is the eleventh verse which states: "For Jehovah God is a sun and a shield: Jehovah will give grace and glory; no good thing will he withheld from them that walk uprightly." It is the Lord who gives both grace and glory or favor and honor. This is what makes worship important. The Lord can be trusted to give us what we need.

The Lord, our God, is the sun. This is the only time that God is called a sun in the whole of the Bible, and it may be that the writers just did not want any confusion with people worshipping the sun. Yet, how beautiful a picture. God is light. In this regard, he is like the sun in power and influence. He lights up the whole of the earth. But, God lights up our lives spirtually as well. Even though men may love darkness, God brings light and with that light, we have life. Just as we cannot live without the sun, so we cannot live without God.

The Lord God is also our shield. The sun may radiate good, but the shield protects us from evil. This is our security and our protection. The ancient warriors wore a shield of brass covered with leather strapped on their arms. It was essential in their battles and for us, God is that essential. Once Martin Luther was asked what he would do if the Duke, his protector, should no longer harbor him. His reply was, "I will take shelter under the broad shield of the Almighty God."

When we think of worship and its great benefits, we can understand the desire to be there. This is why the Psalmist in the long ago could say, "A day in thy courts is better than a thousand. I had rather be a doorkeeper in the house of my God, than to dwell in the tents of wickedness." Several years ago, these were the last words spoken by Alben Barkley, former vice-president of the United States, who was affectionately called, "The Veep." How fitting were these words! But, what about you and me, is this the way we feel?

19. Beginnings

"So teach us to number our days, that we may get us a heart of wisdom."

PSALM 90:12

Beginnings are always important. Whether you are beginning a new year, a new job, a new experience, or just the beginning of another new day, it is something to accept as a great challenge and opportunity. Never again will we have that same unique experience of that particular beginning.

I remember once talking with Dr. Richard Cormier, director of the Chattanooga Symphony Orchestra. I had asked him to make a speech about the symphony to a civic club. While we were visiting before time for him to speak, he said to me, "I just don't know how you preach every Sunday. Where do you find material to use over and over?" I will admit I was a little surprised at his comment, but it also let me know that he was probably better suited for his job than mine, the same as I was better suited for my job than his.

Yet, invariably, when I have thought of some new beginning, my mind has gone back to the 90th Psalm. The superscription about the Psalm tells us that this was a prayer of Moses, one of God's most faithful leaders. There is a beauty and power about this Psalm in dealing with time and the timeless that can be found no where else. It is the ideal for the beginnings in your life.

God Is Eternal

How beautifully the Psalm begins, "Lord, thou hast been our dwelling-place in all generations. Before the mountains were brought forth, or ever thou hadst formed the earth and the world, even from everlasting to everlasting, *thou art God*" (vv. 1, 2).

If you read these words and let them soak in your mind, they have a wonderful calming effect.

What does the Psalmist tell us? First, that the Lord is our dwelling place, generation after generation. He never changes, he is eternal. What a wonderful thing it is to know that when we are frightened or troubled, when we are weary or tired, when we face an unknown future, we can run and find refuge in God. Not only is he always there; he has always been there.

Think of the refuge that he has been in days passed to such characters as Abraham, Isaac, Jacob, Joseph and Moses. He was their strength and their sustainer.

> O God, our help in ages past,
> Our hope for years to come,
> Our shelter from the stormy blasts,
> And our eternal home.
>
> —Isaac Watts

For God, time means nothing, so that the Psalmist can say "a thousand years in thy sight are but as yesterday when it is past." It is even "as a watch in the night."

Man Is Mortal

In contrast to God, man's days are limited; our years are often cut short. There are times when it seems that a person flourishes and then withers right in his prime. We can all say that we have experienced life that has passed away even as a dream or as a sleep. The 10th verse of this Psalm identifies the longevity of man. Our days are numbered at three score and ten (70 years) and even if we have added strength, we are only promised to live 80 years. But even then, our life is soon gone, and we fly away.

One of the reasons that we have to use today for all that it is worth is that we do not have the promise of tomorrow and the reason we must make today count for good, for righteousness, is that this is the only day that we really have to work in. One of my favorite verses in this regard of using today is "This is the day which the Lord hath made; we will rejoice and be glad in it" (Ps. 118:24).

We Must Number Our Days

The secret to using our time well is in learning to number or value our days. We have to pray that God will give us that heart of wisdom. Life is to be lived with the realization that it is something precious; therefore we want to make each day count. The religion of the Bible does not encourage laziness, or putting off until tomorrow what can be done today.

Recently, there has been a little statement that has become popular. It says, "Take time to smell the roses along the way." We can be so busy making a living that we never take time to make a life. We can be so busy with work that we never have time for our children. We can be so busy with things that we forget people.

If you really want to talk to a person who can make each day count, talk to a cancer patient. They know that their life is limited, therefore, they try to squeeze every ounce of living into one 24-hour period. Many of them have accepted their sickness, and they have a calm resolve to live and to love while they have time. And yet, do any of us have any assurance of a long life or many days? Oh, how we need this prayer:

"Teach us to number our days that we may get a heart of wisdom."

Most of us admire the calm resolve of a man like the apostle Paul. His life was useful and full. He made this world a better place in which to live. He glorified Christ. Yet, when he came to the end of the journey here, he could say, "I have fought the good fight, I have finished the course, and I have kept the faith: henceforth there is laid up for me the crown of righteousness, which the Lord, the righteous judge, shall give to me at that day; and not to me only, but also to all them that have loved his appearing" (2 Tim. 4:7-8).

How well are you and I living today and preparing for that tomorrow?

20. Trees

"The righteous shall flourish like the palm tree; he shall grow like a cedar in Lebanon."

PSALM 92:12

I'm sure you remember from high school days, the poem that Sgt. Joyce Kilmer wrote concerning trees. Though he was killed in action, his little poem has lived on as a reminder of the beauty of a tree.

I think that I shall never see
  A poem as lovely as a tree.
A tree whose hungry mouth is pressed
  Against the earth's sweet flowing breast;
A tree that looks at God all day,
  And lifts her leafy arms to pray;
A tree that may in summer wear
  A nest of robins in her hair;
Upon whose bosom the snow has lain;
  Who intimately lives with rain.
Poems are made by fools like me,
  But only God can make a tree.

Perhaps the Psalmist had something like this in mind when he used the picture of a tree to describe the righteous person. He referred to the palm tree and the cedar, and mentioned that they are planted in the house of the Lord. What a beautiful picture this gives us.

The Righteous Pictured

When the Psalmist says that the righteous shall flourish like a palm tree, he is referring to the date palm. The date palm is particularly noted for its stateliness and decorative value. The fruit can be used as a substitute for sugar. The leaves can be used to make mats and baskets. The bark is useful in making rope, while the kernels are used for fodder.

In the long ago, Jericho was called "the city of palm trees." It was a beautiful oasis town near the Dead Sea, and especially refreshing and inviting. We remember that this was the first picture that the children of Israel had of the new and promised land.

We also remember that Deborah, the famous woman judge, sat under a palm tree to dispense her justice to the people. Many years later when Jesus entered the city of Jerusalem riding on the coat of the donkey, the people put palm branches in the road. Others waved them as they shouted, "Hosanna, blessed is He that cometh in the name of the Lord."

The wise man, Solomon, wrote, "Wisdom is a tree of life to them that lay hold upon her" (Prov. 3:18). Jeremiah also used this same imagery as he wrote, "Blessed is the man that trusteth in Jehovah, and whose trust Jehovah is. For he shall be as a tree planted by the waters, that spreadeth out its roots by the river, and shall not fear when heat cometh, but its leaf shall be green; and shall not be careful in the year of drought, neither shall cease from yielding fruit" (Jer. 17:7-8).

But the Psalmist also uses the figure of the righteous as being a cedar of Lebanon. The cedar is noted for its strength, heighth and majesty. It is durable wood, and for this reason, is used in buildings. It is not easily infected by worms due to the resin; it is also suitable for caring; it is the wood that Solomon used in building his temple, and later used in rebuilding the second temple. The branches of the cedar tree are horizontal providing beautiful shade. It is an evergreen, having no time when it is not beautiful and in season.

What a contrast this is to the wicked. The Psalmist says, "The wicked spring as the grass, and when all the workers of iniquity do flourish; it is that they shall be destroyed for ever" (v. 7).

The real point in all of this is that each of us can be like a tree in our righteousness. We can be as children of God—a people for all seasons. We can be ever green and fertile and fruitbearing. We, too, can flourish in the courts of our God.

Their Fruit

The Psalmist points to one reason for their steadfastness and security. It is that they are planted in the house of God and because of this, they bring forth fruit, since they are full of sap. As Christians, we are to be fruitbearing people. We are in a dangerous position when we no longer bear fruit, and can be completely cutoff.

Jesus said, "Herein is my Father glorified, that ye bear much fruit; and so shall ye be my disciples" (John 15:8).

The fruit that we bear is the way that we live daily. We can influence others for good; we can win souls to the Master, we can tell the good news of salvation. The beauty is that we can bring forth fruit even in old age. This certainly happened to Moses, when even at 120, he was serving the Lord productively.

The results of all of this will be that our work will show that God is upright. Our confidence will be in him since he is our rock or strength. How wonderful to know that we can live a righteous life and be "full of sap and green."

What kind of tree are you in God's sight?

21. Sing

"Oh come, let us sing unto Jehovah; let us make a joyful noise to the rock of our salvation."

PSALM 95:1

When we remember that the Psalms were used as the singing book of Israel, we can easily see how the 95th one fits into place. It is thought that this particular Psalm was written following the exile in Babylon. It calls upon the people for two important ideas.

Acceptable Worship

It would be a good idea if every Christian had a hymn book in his house. That way, he could go to his songbook daily, meditate upon the words of many songs, and sing some of the songs during his daily activities. It is good to sing to the Lord. There needs to be times in our life when we make joyful noices.

Singing in worship plays a vital role in the worship of God. We need to remember that singing is not really a call to worship, but it is indeed worship itself. The Psalms are full of expressions that indicate how we ought to sing. For instance:

Oh sing unto Jehovah a new song;
For he hath done marvelous things:
His right hand, and his holy arm,
Hath wrought salvation for him.
Jehovah hath made known his salvation:

His righteousness hath he openly showed
in the sight of the nations.
Psalm 98:1-2

Oh sing unto Jehovah a new song;
Sing unto Jehovah, all the earth.
Sing unto Jehovah, bless his name;
Show forth his salvation from day to day.
Psalm 96:1-2

Sing aloud unto God our strength:
Make a joyful noise unto the God of Jacob.
Psalm 81:1

Oh clap your hands, all ye peoples;
Shout unto God with the voice of triumph. . . .
Sing praises to God, sing praises:
Sing praises unto our King, sing praises.
For God is the King of all the earth:
Sing ye praises with understanding.
Psalm 47:1, 6-7

These are but a few examples of the many times that the Psalms tell us to sing. It should be noted, in particular, that the whole book closes with five Psalms that all begin "Praise ye Jehovah" (Pss. 146-150).

We are told that the Jews used a Psalm daily for the sacrifices in Jerusalem. On the first day, the 24th Psalm was sung. On the second day, the 48th Psalm was used. On the third day, the 82nd Psalm was used for praise and worship. On the fourth day, the 94th Psalm was sung. On the fifth day, the 81st Psalm was used. On the sixth day, the 93rd Psalm was the worship idea. And finally, on the seventh day, the Sabbath, both Psalm 38 and 92 were sung. This kept before the people the idea of God and the fact that he was due worship. They worshipped God in song because it was to be a joyful, happy experience.

The whole concept behind the word "worship" is to bind a person back. In this sense, it means to bind one back to God, his creator. The Psalmist says, "For Jehovah is a great God, and a great King above all gods." We understand that this means that God made all this world and that he owns it. We as his creatures are to worship him. Therefore, the appeal the Psalmist makes is this, "O come, let us worship and bow down; let us kneel before Jehovah our Maker: for he is our God, and we are the people of his pasture, and the sheep of his hand" (vv. 6, 7).

A Warning from the Lord

But the Psalmist is aware that more than songs of praise are needed. The people must follow worship with earnest obedience and acceptance of his will. Therefore, the Psalmist gives an urgent warning from the Lord. He calls upon all of us in these words, "Today, oh that ye would hear his voice! Harden not your heart. . . ." (vv. 7-8).

The biggest problem with most of us in hearing the voice of God is the folly of procrastination. We hear, but do not respond. If we can put it off another day or another week or even another year. It's so easy to forget the urgency of living today for God, and for us in the Christian age, for his son.

The Psalmist refers back to the history of the Israelites. He reminds all of us not to harden our hearts as the people did at Meribah in the long ago. This story, found in Exodus 17, tells us that the people came to Moses murmuring and complaining about the lack of water. Time and again, God had shown them his blessing and providential care, but they so easily forgot. Moses told the people that he would stand before them and smite the rock. Water came gushing forth that was plentiful, but the name Meribah was given to the location because of the people's chiding and striving.

The other references to Massah, an experience in the wilderness, are related in Numbers 20. It was here that the people again complained against Moses and his leadership. Moses lifted up his hand and smote the rock twice, and the water came forth abundantly. The sad thing about Massah, which means strife, is that Moses became angered and showed his impatience by adding his own honor and glory to the deed. He said, "Hear now, ye rebels: shall we bring you forth water out of this rock?" His sin was that he had not magnified God in the eyes of the people. Because of this temptation and sin, he did not enter the promised land. Yet, we would have to add, that the people who had tempted the Lord and provoked him had to wander in the wilderness for 40 years because of the lack of their faith.

What a lesson for us today. A warning that our hearts must not be hardened. We, too, have a land of rest, the promised land of heaven, so much greater even than Canaan.

22. Praise

"Make a joyful noise unto the Lord, all ye lands. Serve the Lord with gladness; come before his presence with singing."

PSALM 100:1-2

It happened in New York on a cold, blustery evening. A little girl of ten, with her younger brother, was trying to sell some cheap trinkets at a busy intersection. Huddled together, yet still shivering, they captured the sympathy of a wealthy lady who invited them to her penthouse for hot chocolate. As they stepped inside, tracking the carpet with their wet feet, the children's eyes surveyed the room with its beautiful paintings, draperies and furnishings. When they were served the hot chocolate in cups that matched the saucers, it was evident that they were further amazed.

Finally, the little girl blurted out the question, "Lady, are you God's wife?"

"Why no," she replied. "What made you ask?"

"Because," the little girl answered softly, "You are so kind to us."

As the children prepared to leave, their benefactor decided to give them some food and clothing to take home. She resolved when they were gone, to let their footprints stay on her carpet awhile as a reminder of what had happened. This experience led her to be more thankful.

There are two classes of people—those who take everything for granted and those who take everything with gratitude.

The 100th Psalm has long been associated with thanksgiving and praise. The Doxology is sung to a hymn tune that we call OLD HUNDRED.

Praise God from whom all blessings flow,
Praise Him all creatures here below,
Praise Him above ye Heavenly hosts,
Praise Father, Son and Holy Ghost.

Possibly, the 100th Psalm was used in connection with the Feast of the Wheat Harvest. This was the time of the year when the people came to give thanks for all that God had blessed them with, not only through the year, but especially at the harvest season. It is good to have time set aside to praise God and give thanks to him.

Praising God

The people were instructed to make a joyful noise unto the Lord. This idea was in connection with temple worship; it was worship that was to be entered into joyfully. All lands were invited to participate in such praise. It was to be universal. In some ways, this anticipated the coming of Christianity, which, as one of its purposes, brings all people together in Christ.

John, while on the isle of Patmos, heard the four living creatures and the twenty-four elders singing this new song to the Lamb, "Worthy art thou to take the book, and to open the seals thereof: for thou wast slain, and didst purchase unto God with thy blood men of every tribe, and tongue, and people, and nation, and madest them to be unto our God a kingdom and priests; and they reign upon the earth" (Rev. 5:9-10).

The people were also to serve the Lord with gladness. Gladness is largely a matter of attitude. You can either view worship as a burden or as a joy, but it all depends on you. One of the most remarkable statements in the Bible is the fact that Paul, while in prison, could write to the Philippian Christians and say, "Rejoice in the Lord always: again I say, Rejoice" (Phil. 4:4). It ought to be a characteristic of every Christian to be joyful and glad.

Jesus told the woman at the well that God is a spirit, and he desired worship that is in spirit and in truth. The spirit, or attitude, is vital. If you enter into singing and giving and listening to God's word with great joy and cheerfulness, you will be blessed.

They were to come before God's presence with singing. In the Old Testament, God had commanded that people were to sing. We have the example of Miriam and the women singing after they crossed the Red Sea (Exod. 15). Deborah and Barak sang a song of victory after defeating Sisera (Judg. 5). Even when David killed Goliath, the women sang (1 Sam. 18:6-7).

Certainly, we are authorized to sing in the New Testament. The Bible indicates that we are to sing and make melody in our hearts to the Lord (Eph. 5:19). Paul said simply, "I will sing with the spirit, and I will sing with the understanding also" (1 Cor. 14:15).

Knowing God

The Jew, as well as the Christian, must acknowledge that Jehovah is God. The Psalmist says, "Know ye that Jehovah, He is God; it is He that hath made us, and we are His." We confess that the god of the Bible is the true God, the God of history and the God of redemption. I believe in the God who so loved the world that he gave us his son. This is the essence of faith; to believe that the Lord is God (Heb. 11:6).

It's good for us to remember that God is our creator. We know that he made all things in the world, but let's never forget that he also made us. We are his sheep, and he will be our shepherd, but more than this, we are his people, and he will take care of us.

Finally, we must remember that "the Lord is good; his mercy endureth forever." You remember as a child saying the little prayer, "God is great and God is good, let us thank him for our food." Yes, we need to remember his goodness. His mercy and faithfulness endure forever, and we can depend on this.

23. Thanksgiving

"Bless Jehovah, O my soul, and forget not all his benefits."

PSALM 103:2

I firmly believe that if you will *think,* you will *thank.* The biblical injunction is simply in everything give thanks (1 Thess. 5:18). Certainly, the 103rd Psalm is a psalm that teaches the idea of thanksgiving.

The Thankfulness for All Benefits

The Psalmist says that we are to thank God and bless him for all of his gifts. It is to be an expression that involves our whole being. Instead of asking for a blessing, the Psalmist teaches that we should bless him.

This is certainly true in connection with the pilgrim fathers, and the great hardships they endured. In 1621, they paused to give thanks for survival in the new world. They placed five grains of corn on the table at each place to remind themselves of how meager were the things that they had. Yet God had sustained them and blessed them.

The Psalmist lists some things for which we should give thanks. First, God forgives us all our sins. The Psalmist says a little later, "as far as the east is from the west, so far hath he removed our transgressions from us" (v. 12). The interesting fact about this is that the Psalmist does not use the north or the south as the measuring distance, for it is possible to come to the end of our earth at the Poles. But this is not true of the east and the west, for we can continue to go completely around the world. Good for those of us who are Christians is the fact that this kind of idea was taught in the Old Testament, but we have a greater power and force through Jesus Christ our Lord. The Bible teaches that he cleanses us from all sins as we walk in the light of his truth and grace (1 John 1:7).

Second, God heals all of our diseases. What a wonderful thing that we have the power of prayer, that we can take our problems to the Lord. In times of great hardship and crisis, we can ask the Lord's help. We have a balm in Gilead, for we know the great physician. I would hate to think what the world would be like if we could not pray to God in time of illness. But often we fail to thank him for blessings that we have received when we have been healed. It is just as important to bless the name of the Lord for benefits received as it is to request them.

Third, God redeems our life from destruction. Though we may not be exactly sure what kind of destruction the Psalmist was talking about in his day, we know that there is the destruction that awaits the evil people. How thankful we ought to be for a God who gives us salvation and hope and life in the world to come. We need to be grateful and thankful for his goodness.

Fourth, he crowns us with loving kindness and tender mercy more than we ever deserve. We are continually surrounded with God's grace.

Finally, the Psalmist says we should give thanks because God satisfies our desire with good things. He may not always give us what we want, but he does give us what we need. We can be renewed like the eagle and go forward in faith.

The Nature of God

The reason that we can be so thankful to God is that he is ever gracious and good to us. The qualities of God are also presented in this Psalm. God always does right.

He is merciful and gracious, that is why he has worked out a plan for our salvation. He is slow to anger and is patient, his loving kindness is abundant.

But, perhaps, the best picture to think of God is what the Psalmist uses here in verse 13, "Like as a father pitieth his children, so Jehovah pitieth them that fear him." God is our father, he understands us, loves us, and even corrects us. It is so easy in this picture to think of your own father and how understanding he was with you as a child, and how he tried to teach you. What a wonderful thing it was when I was allowed to go to my father's place of work. How thrilling and exciting it was to be with him. Even to ride the elevator in his building, was something that brought delight. If a human father can love us so much and bring joy to our lives, think of what the Heavenly Father can do for us. God does pity us as his children, it is wonderful to say that we are his. Is it any wonder that John the apostle wrote, "Behold what manner of love the Father hath bestowed upon us, that we should be called children of God; and such we are. . . . Beloved, now are we children of God, and it is not yet made manifest what we shall be" (1 John 3:1-2).

God is eternal. Therefore, we can place our trust in him, for he will always be the same. His righteousness is extended to those who obey him and keep his covenant.

The Psalm closes with all the hosts of God and all of his works praising and blessing his name. The obvious is that man—you and I—should bless him, too. The old song suggests "Count your many blessings, name them one by one, and it will surprise you what the Lord hath done."

W. E. Sangster tells of one of his visits as a minister to a hospital where a child was strapped to a box, suffering from a curved spine. Her bed was beside a window. After he spoke to her, she cheerfully said, "Do you want to play a game with me?"

"What game, child?" Dr. Sangster responded.

"Oh, a game of the stars," she proclaimed. "They are just ready to come out. I name all the people I love, like Mommie and Daddy and my dog and let a star represent them. But," she continued, "there are not enough stars to go around."

You and I had better go home and count the stars.

24. Help

> "I will lift up mine eyes unto the mountains; from whence shall my help come? My help cometh from the Lord, who made heaven and earth."
>
> PSALM 121:1-2

I would like for you to picture a scene of pilgrims climbing Mount Zion, the holy hill of God. As far as your eye can see, there are travelers, of all ages, who represent loyal Jews, who are making an annual pilgrimage to worship God in his holy place. As they come along, winding their way ever higher, they are singing and happy. What a wonderful feeling they have! How we admire them—these people who are praising God even for the opportunity of getting to worship him.

The 121st Psalm, long a favorite of many people, is one of fifteen songs of ascents or degrees. Many Bible students think they were written during the exile when the Jews were thinking about Jerusalem and home. But I believe that they were the songs used on the way to the city of Jerusalem as the people worshipped God. The whole group of them is found from Psalm 120 to 134.

The Call of the Hills

How thrilling and majestic is the line, "I will lift up mine eyes unto the mountains." There is a majesty and serenity about the mountains, as they represent aspiration. I remember reading of William O. Douglas, who took up mountain climbing to strengthen that leg after he had injured it in an accident. This is almost indicative of man's desire to achieve and to go forward. There are many great mountains in biblical history. We think of Noah and the ark that landed at Mount Ararat, of the Israelites as they surrounded Mount Sinai and heard God's law, of Moses standing on Mount Pisgah, looking as far as his eye could see at the Promised Land, and of Elijah and his famous contest with the false prophets at Mount Carmel. It's easy to remember Jesus, in connection with the Sermon on the Mount, his transfiguration on another mountain, and his oft going to the Mount of Olives. Sometimes, it is not physical mountains that we can see but beyond our natural sight, the loftiness of God. As the Jews spoke these words, they were thinking of God and of home. I think today, you and I can lift up our eyes to the mountains and see God.

We long in our weary world for help. Real help comes only from God. He is identified here as the one who made the heavens and the earth, He's not merely a travelled deity, but the God of the whole world. The help that comes from God who made the mountains suggests for us peace and beauty and stability. When God sends help, the spirit finds rest; his help means moral health and vigor.

The Reality of God in Our Daily Lives

The Psalmist declares, "The Lord is thy keeper!" He is called the "keeper of Israel," of a particular nation of people, but he is also the keeper of individuals. Once a little girl on board a ship did not seem troubled because there was a storm raging. Some of the passengers asked her, "Why are you not afraid?" She replied, "I'm not afraid because my Father is the Captain. He will guide me safely through this storm."

You and I need to remember that as we go through life, there are many perils and pitfalls, even as there were as these ancient pilgrims made their journey to Jerusalem.

Yet God is aware of anyone of them, and he will protect us. The promise says he will not suffer thy foot to be moved. How wonderful that we have a God who is our keeper. He gives us daily help and strength, both as we go out from our home and as we come back at the end of day. In this connection, don't you appreciate the words of the Lord Jesus: "And lo, I am with you *always*, even to the end of the world" (Matt. 28:20).

The Psalmist also says "The Lord is thy shade upon thy right hand." God does not sleep, for he guards us continually. It is true that sentries had to be posted in the camps of the people who were on these pilgrimages. And so taking that idea of the sentry, the Psalmist thinks that God is like an eternal sentinal. He does not take a vacation from our watchcare; he does not slumber nor sleep; he is continually watching and caring for us; he knows our every need.

Finally, the Psalmist says the Lord is thy preserver. He will keep us from all evil. It's wonderful that we can pray. "Lead us not into temptation, but deliver us from evil." We have the assurance that God will be there for us. Not only will he preserve us from evil, the promise is he will preserve our souls. He will provide for us an eternal home so that we never have to worry about any cares or afflictions, or disappointments. As the wise man, Solomon, said concerning our death, "And the dust returneth to the earth as it was, and the spirit returneth unto God who gave it" (Eccl. 12:7).

This wonderful Psalm teaches us that we must get a vision of God. We must come to realize and understand that God is present and at work in our lives. We do not live alone. He is there to help us.

Unto the hills around do I lift up
  My longing eyes;
Oh, whence for me shall my salvation come,

From whence arise?

From God, the Lord, doth come my certain aid,
From God, the Lord, who heaven and earth hath made.

From every evil shall He keep thy soul,
From every sin;
Jehovah shall preserve thy going out,
Thy coming in;

Above thee watching, He whom we adore,
Shall keep thee henceforth, yea, forevermore.

25. Search

> "Search me, O God, and know my heart: try me, and know my thoughts."
>
> PSALM 139:23

Have you ever had the feeling that you were unhappy where you were, or that no one understood your problem? You may have thought many times that you would like to get away from the rat race. You may have thought if you could just fly away and be gone, that there would be no problems. Or you may have felt that you are not appreciated where you are, and that if you could just go to where people really understood your worth and value—you would be appreciated. Or perhaps you even have felt that no one understands the needs of your heart.

If this is so, you need to know that God is interested in you. There is someone who cares. The 139th Psalm was written for you. It is one of the greatest Psalms in the whole book.

The Omniscience of God

The Psalmist begins, "O Jehovah, thou hast searched me, and known me." You can't help but notice how personal this is. It's not that God knows all of us, he knows *me*. Where can I go where God would not know me and be concerned about me. He searches me and he knows me.

I like the story of the little boy who was on his way to worship. He was stopped by an older man who asked him where he was going. The little boy replied, "I'm on my way to worship God."

Then the man said, "Is your God a big God or a little God?" The boy's reply was a classic, "He is so big that the heavens cannot hold him, but he is so small that he lives in my heart."

The Psalmist said that God knows my downsitting and my uprising. God is the first one to say "Good Morning" to me each day. He begins and ends your day. Do you ever take time to thank him for this?

Do You Remember Him?

God knows your thoughts even from afar. God knows all of our ways, the times when we are blue, and the times when we are on the mountain tops.

He searches out our path and knows of our lying down. He knows our thoughts even before we form them into words. He is behind us and before us. There is no escape from God. Jonah learned this lesson in the long ago. He tried to run away from God, thinking that God could not be out on the mighty Mediterranean Sea. But even there, God knew where Jonah was. He prepared a great storm and then a great fish to make this reluctant prophet aware that God knew where he was.

It seems to me that we can remember this idea easier if we think of a mother and a baby. A mother knows everything about that baby. She looks at him, nurses him, rocks him, and holds him. She measures his feet and his body. She knows the slightest change that comes day by day. Why? Because she loves the baby. In the same way, God loves us. He is like a mother to us. He searches us and knows us out of interest. He is concerned.

Jesus told us, on one occasion, that God knows even when a sparrow falls, and that the very hairs of our head are numbered (Luke 12:6-7).

I read once of a man who thought the world was in such terrible condition, that he prayed, "Lord, have you seen the morning *Times*?" Certainly, he didn't seem to be aware that God knew not only what was in the paper, but he knew before it was even printed. There is no power or force on earth that can separate us from God's command. We take pleasure in the fact that we can make such an affirmation as this, "For I am persuaded that neither death, nor life, nor angels, nor principalities, nor things present, nor things to come, nor powers, nor heights, nor depth, nor any other creature, shall be able to separate us from the love of God, which is in Christ Jesus our Lord" (Rom. 8:38-39).

The Presence and Love of God

Coupled with the knowledge of God is the ever presence of God surrounding us with love. The Psalmist asks, "Whither shall I go from thy spirit? Or whither shall I flee from thy presence?" Then the Psalmist tried to imagine where he could escape from God. He tried to ascend into the heavens or to descend into the place of the dead, but God was there. He tried to take the wings of the morning or even to dwell in the uttermost parts of the sea, but God was still there.

The expression "the wings of the morning" is interesting because the Psalmist is talking about the earliest dawning of the day. The velocity of light is great, and if we could take wings and be gone, even as the morning comes, it would seem at times wonderful. But the significant thing is that there is no place that we can go, not even the darkness of night, that can remove us from the presence of God.

It is knowledge that God is ever present that causes the Psalmist to say, "For such knowledge is too wonderful for me, it is high, I cannot attain unto it" (v. 7).

In this connection, we recall the words of John Greenleaf Whittier,

> I know not where His islands lift,
> Their fronded palms in air;
> I only know I cannot drift,
> Beyond His love and care.

It is God's great concern that causes him to want to save us. His love is manifested to us in sending our Savior.

God, Our Maker

Two of the most important verses in the entire Psalm are verses 13 and 14. The Psalmist here acknowledges that God is his maker.

"For thou didst form my inward parts: thou didst cover me in my mother's womb." This expression tells us that God's care and concern began with the creation of each person in his mother's womb. God covered me with sinews and flesh and gave me bones and blood, even in that prenatal state. It's a mystery, yet it's wonderful.

The idea of covering me could also be like weaving together strands of material to make a basket, or knitting together thread to make a garment. God has knit me together and woven me together, and I am a unique person.

Life begins in the mother's womb. There is breathing, the formation of hands and feet, and the sustaining of life with the food received from the mother. With this being so, abortion for just any reason should not be a norm. How thankful I am that Mary, the mother of our Lord, did not believe in abortion. If she had, we could say that there Emanuel is in the trash can!

The Psalmist says, "I will give thanks unto thee; for I am fearfully and wonderfully made: wonderful are thy works; and that my soul knoweth right well."

We should say this over and over and give thanks to God for our being fearfully and wonderfully made. We come into this world as infants, but God gives us the power to grow and to change in childhood and then into adolescence and finally into mature adults. We see all the parts of our life coming together, and we know that God is interested in us. We can attest to the fact that we are wonderfully made.

The Psalmist tells us that his frame was not made in secret, nor hidden from God, but all the days of his life, God had been interested in him. He says, "How precious also are thy thoughts unto me, O God! How great is the sum of them!" If we had to take all the things that God has done for us up to our lives to this point, couldn't we say that God has been good to us? If we had a count of them, the sum would be great.

The Psalm closes just about like it began. He acknowledges at the beginning that God does search and know us. But he closes with the prayer, "Search me, O God, and know my heart." Why does he want such searching? He wants to see if there is any wicked way so that this can be removed, and he can be led in the way that's everlasting.

John Short of Toronto tells the story of a young man who came to church everyday at lunch time and had a brief prayer. Curious as to what the young man would say, the preacher got close enough to hear him, and he said simply, "Jesus, it's Jimmie." Later, the preacher was called to this boy's bedside as he was dying, and he felt the life going out of the boy. When this happened, the preacher said, "I could almost hear the words, and so I repeated them, 'Jimmie, it's Jesus.' "

Our Lord searches us, tries us, is interested in us because of that everlasting home.

As a mother stills her child,
  Thou canst hush the ocean wild;
Boisterous waves obey thy will,
  When thou sayest to them, "Be still,"
Wonderous sovereign of the sea,
  Jesus, Savior, pilot me.